Company's Coming®

Greatest Hits

Italian

companyscoming.com
visit our web-site

Over 175 best-selling recipes

GREATEST HITS SERIES

Italian

Second printing April 2004

Canadian Cataloguing in Publication Data
Paré, Jean
    Italian

(Greatest hits series)
Author: Jean Paré
Includes index.
ISBN 1-895455-53-7

    1. Cookery, Italian. I. Title. II. Series: Paré, Jean.
Greatest hits series.

TX723.P29 2001   641.5945   C00-901615-5

Published by
Company's Coming Publishing Limited
2311 – 96 Street, Edmonton, Alberta,
Canada T6N 1G3
Tel: 780 • 450-6223
Fax: 780 • 450-1857
www.companyscoming.com

Company's Coming is a registered trademark owned by Company's Coming Publishing Limited

Printed in China

FRONT COVER:
1. Italian Cheesecake, page 113
2. Seafood Italia, page 45
3. Bruschetta, page 7
4. Vegetable Pasta Salad, page 14

Props Courtesy Of: The Bay

companyscoming.com
visit our web-site

table of contents

our cookbooks

COMPANY'S COMING SERIES

150 Delicious Squares
Casseroles
Muffins & More
Salads
Appetizers
Soups & Sandwiches
Cookies
Pasta
Barbecues
Preserves
Chicken, Etc.
Kids Cooking
Cooking For Two
Breakfasts & Brunches
Slow Cooker Recipes
One-Dish Meals
Starters
Stir-Fry
Make-Ahead Meals

The Potato Book
Low-Fat Cooking
Low-Fat Pasta
Cook For Kids
Stews, Chilies & Chowders
Fondues
The Beef Book
Asian Cooking
The Cheese Book
The Rookie Cook
Rush-Hour Recipes
Sweet Cravings
Year-Round Grilling
Garden Greens
Chinese Cooking
The Pork Book
Recipes for Leftovers
The Egg Book
◄NEW► *May 1/04*

GREATEST HITS SERIES

Italian
Mexican

LIFESTYLE SERIES

Grilling
Diabetic Cooking
Heart-Friendly Cooking
Diabetic Dinners

MOST LOVED SERIES

Most Loved Appetizers
Most Loved Main Courses
◄NEW► *Apr 1/04*

SPECIAL OCCASIONS SERIES

Gifts from the Kitchen
Cooking for the Seasons
Home for the Holidays
Weekend Cooking
Decadent Desserts

company's coming story

ean Paré grew up understanding that the combination of family, friends and home cooking is the essence of a good life. From her mother she learned to appreciate good cooking, while her father praised even her earliest attempts. When she left home she took with her many acquired family recipes, a love of cooking and an intriguing desire to read recipe books like novels!

In 1963, when her four children had all reached school age, Jean volunteered to cater the 50th anniversary of the Vermilion School of Agriculture, now Lakeland College. Working out of her home, Jean prepared a dinner for over 1000 people which launched a flourishing catering operation that continued for over eighteen years. During that time she was provided with countless opportunities to test new ideas with immediate feedback—resulting in empty plates and contented customers! Whether preparing cocktail sandwiches for a house party or serving a hot meal for 1500 people, Jean Paré earned a reputation for good food, courteous service and reasonable prices.

"Why don't you write a cookbook?" Time and again, as requests for her recipes mounted, Jean was asked that question. Jean's response was to team up with her son, Grant Lovig, in the fall of 1980 to form Company's Coming Publishing Limited. April 14, 1981, marked the debut of "150 DELICIOUS SQUARES," the first Company's Coming cookbook in what soon would become Canada's most popular cookbook series.

Jean Paré's operation has grown steadily from the early days of working out of a spare bedroom in her home. Full-time staff includes marketing personnel located in major cities across Canada. Home Office is based in Edmonton, Alberta in a modern building constructed specially for the company.

Today the company distributes throughout Canada and the United States in addition to numerous overseas markets, all under the guidance of Jean's daughter, Gail Lovig. Best-sellers many times over in English, Company's Coming cookbooks have also been published in French and Spanish. Familiar and trusted in home kitchens around the world, Company's Coming cookbooks are offered in a variety of formats, including the original softcover series.

Jean Paré's approach to cooking has always called for quick and easy recipes using everyday ingredients. Even when traveling, she is constantly on the lookout for new ideas to share with her readers. At home, she can usually be found researching and writing recipes, or working in the company's test kitchen. Jean continues to gain new supporters by adhering to what she calls "the golden rule of cooking:" never share a recipe you wouldn't use yourself. It's an approach that works—*millions of times over!*

foreword

f you think garlic, tomato sauce and pasta are the perfect combination, then *Italian* is the book to reach for! With over 160 recipes in this collection, each has been tested to measure up to your taste buds.

Italian fare—everything from spaghetti and meatballs to pizza—has garnered fans of all ages. Make home-made pasta for a special dinner with friends or keep it simple with commercial pasta on a weeknight with family. Whichever you choose, there is a multitude of sauces to dress it up with, not to mention a variety of vegetables and meats.

For a special breakfast or brunch, whip up some eggs into one of several frittatas, including Zucchini Frittata or Red-Topped Frittata. For a hearty lunch, try Italian Minestrone that's chock full of vegetables or Tortellini Soup.

If guests are on their way, Bruschetta is an easy and delicious appetizer. Start your meal with Artichoke Salad or Prosciutto And Melon Salad— or have either one as a main course.

Italian includes Basic Pizza Crust, but there are several creative versions too, such as Orzo Pizza Crust. From there, go on to make Pesto, Chicken and Pepper Focaccia, either as an after-game snack or as dinner. Shrimp Tetrazzini, makes an easy main course, while Creamy Mussels 'N' Pasta, is a rich-tasting meal.

To top any meal off in an extraordinary way, create Bocconne Dolce, a luscious concoction of meringue, chocolate, fruit and cream. Afterwards, or even for a mid-day coffee break, a batch of Choco-Choco Chip Biscotti is so impressive you'll always want some on hand. With recipes from *Italian*, everyone will say "bravo"!

each recipe

Each recipe has been analyzed using the most up-to-date version of the Canadian Nutrient File from Health Canada, which is based on the United States Department of Agriculture (USDA) Nutrient Database. If more than one ingredient is listed (such as "hard margarine or butter"), then the first ingredient is used in the analysis. Where an ingredient reads "sprinkle," "optional," or "for garnish," it is not included as part of the nutrition information.

Margaret Ng, B.Sc. (Hon), M.A.
Registered Dietician

★★★★★★★★★★★★★★★★★★★★★★★★★★★★★★★★

Appetizers

Quell the hunger pangs until dinner time with any of these fabulous Italian starters! Fried Mozzarella, page 9, or Little Stuffed Tomatoes, page 10, are perfect for packing a big punch of flavor in a small package. Put out a plate of Antipasto, page 12, and let guests take their pick of tasty tidbits.

BRUSCHETTA

Bruschetta (broo-SKEH-tah) is from the Italian word that means "to roast over coals." Only 20 minutes preparation time.

Large roma (plum) tomatoes, seeded and diced	5-6	5-6
Garlic cloves, crushed	2	2
Finely chopped fresh sweet basil	¼ cup	60 mL
Olive oil	2 tbsp.	30 mL
Red wine vinegar	2 tbsp.	30 mL
Salt	1 tsp.	5 mL
Freshly ground pepper	¼ tsp.	1 mL
Baguette slices, 1 inch (2.5 cm) each, lightly toasted on 1 side	15	15
Grated fresh Parmesan cheese	2 tbsp.	30 mL

Combine first 7 ingredients in medium bowl. Cover. Let stand at room temperature for at least 2 hours to allow flavors to blend. Drain.

Divide tomato mixture among untoasted sides of bread slices.

Sprinkle each with equal amount of Parmesan cheese. Place on ungreased baking sheet. Broil 6 to 8 inches (15 to 20 cm) from heat until edges are golden. Makes 15 bruschetta.

1 bruschetta: 133 Calories; 3.3 g Total Fat; 405 mg Sodium; 4 g Protein; 22 g Carbohydrate; 1 g Dietary Fiber

Pictured on front cover.

BRUSCHETTA PIZZA

An attractive twist to bruschetta. Colorful with flavor to match.

BASIC PIZZA CRUST

All-purpose flour	1½ cups	375 mL
Instant yeast	1¼ tsp.	6 mL
Salt	¼ tsp.	1 mL
Cooking oil	2 tbsp.	30 mL
Very warm water	½ cup	125 mL

TOPPING

Salad dressing (or mayonnaise)	½ cup	125 mL
Grated Parmesan cheese	¼ cup	60 mL
Dried whole oregano	1 tsp.	5 mL
Dried sweet basil	½ tsp.	2 mL
Pepper	½ tsp.	2 mL
Garlic cloves, minced (or ½ tsp., 2 mL, garlic powder), optional	2	2
Chopped pitted ripe olives	⅓ cup	75 mL
Roma (plum) tomatoes, seeded and diced	3	3
Grated part-skim mozzarella cheese	1½ cups	375 mL

Basic Pizza Crust: Put flour, yeast and salt into food processor fitted with dough blade. With machine running, pour cooking oil and warm water through feed tube. Process for about 30 seconds. Cover. Let dough rest for 15 minutes. Roll out on lightly floured surface. Press in greased 12 inch (30 cm) pizza pan or 9 x 13 inch (22 x 33 cm) pan. Poke holes all over crust, except edge, with fork. Bake on bottom rack in 425°F (220°C) oven for 8 minutes. Press down any bulges. Cool slightly.

Topping: Mix first 6 ingredients in medium bowl. Spread on crust.

Sprinkle with olives, tomato and mozzarella cheese. Bake for about 8 minutes. Cuts into 16 long thin appetizer wedges or 24 squares.

1 wedge: 144 Calories; 8.3 g Total Fat; 193 mg Sodium; 5 g Protein; 12 g Carbohydrate; 1 g Dietary Fiber

TOMATO SALSA SAUCE

Make lots of this when tomato crops are plentiful. Freeze in cartons to always have on hand. Use for spaghetti or pizza sauce.

Chopped onion	1 cup	250 mL
Finely chopped garlic	1 tbsp.	15 mL
Olive oil	3 tbsp.	50 mL
Peeled, coarsely chopped tomatoes	5 cups	1.25 L
Can of tomato paste	5½ oz.	156 mL
Bay leaves	2-3	2-3
Dried sweet basil	1½ tsp.	7 mL
Dried whole oregano	1½ tsp.	7 mL
Granulated sugar	2 tsp.	10 mL
Salt	1½ tsp.	7 mL
Pepper	½ tsp.	2 mL

Sauté onion and garlic in olive oil in large saucepan until soft.

Add remaining 8 ingredients. Stir. Bring to a boil. Reduce heat. Simmer, uncovered, for 1¼ to 2 hours until desired consistency. Stir occasionally. Discard bay leaves. Makes about 2¾ cups (675 mL).

¼ cup (60 mL): 72 Calories; 4.2 g Total Fat; 390 mg Sodium; 1 g Protein; 9 g Carbohydrate; 2 g Dietary Fiber

---

To retain as much juice as possible from tomatoes, slice from top to bottom instead of crosswise.

FRIED MOZZARELLA

Strips or triangles of cheese deep-fried with a crumb coating.

Mozzarella cheese slices (see Note)	16	16
All-purpose flour	⅓ cup	75 mL
Large eggs	2	2
Water	4 tsp.	20 mL
Salt	¼ tsp.	1 mL
Pepper	¹⁄₁₆ tsp.	0.5 mL
Fine dry bread crumbs	1 cup	250 mL

Cooking oil, for deep-frying

Separate cheese slices into groups of 4, keeping slices in each group tightly together. Cut each group in half through center, then in half again making 4 thick strips. Repeat with remaining cheese, making 16 strips in total. Triangles may be made by cutting cornerwise.

Measure flour into flat dish.

Combine eggs, water, salt and pepper in cereal bowl. Beat with fork until blended.

Line baking sheet with waxed paper. Measure bread crumbs into another flat dish. Dip cheese strips into flour, then egg mixture. Completely cover with bread crumbs. Lay cheese on waxed paper. Chill for 1 hour or more.

Deep-fry, a few strips at a time, in 375°F (190°C) cooking oil, browning both sides. Carefully remove with slotted spoon to drain on paper towels. Makes 16 mozzarella sticks.

2 sticks: 163 Calories; 10.1 g Total Fat; 645 mg Sodium; 9 g Protein; 9 g Carbohydrate; trace Dietary Fiber

Pictured on page 17.

Note: A solid piece of mozzarella may be used instead. Try to cut uniform slices.

PITA PIZZAS

Serve whole pitas as an individual lunch or snack.

Lean ground beef	½ lb.	225 g
Finely diced onion	⅓ cup	75 mL
Ground oregano	¼ tsp.	1 mL
Salt	¼ tsp.	1 mL
Garlic powder	¼ tsp.	1 mL
Whole wheat pita breads (7 inch, 18 cm, size)	8	8
Can of tomato (or pizza) sauce	7½ oz.	213 mL
Finely chopped fresh mushrooms	1 cup	250 mL
Finely diced green pepper	1½ cups	375 mL
Grated part-skim mozzarella cheese	2 cups	500 mL

Scramble-fry ground beef, onion, oregano, salt and garlic powder in non-stick frying pan until no pink remains in beef and onion is soft. Drain.

Flatten pita breads with rolling pin. Spread each pita bread with 1½ tbsp. (25 mL) tomato sauce. Sprinkle with 3 tbsp. (50 mL) beef mixture, 2 tbsp. (30 mL) mushrooms and 2 tbsp. (30 mL) green pepper. Sprinkle ¼ cup (60 mL) cheese over top. Broil 6 to 8 inches (15 to 20 cm) from heat until edges are crusty and cheese is melted. Cuts into 8 wedges each, for a total of 64.

1 wedge: 301 Calories; 8 g Total Fat; 544 mg Sodium; 19 g Protein; 39 g Carbohydrate; 5 g Dietary Fiber

To refresh a dry pita, lightly spray with water on both sides. Microwave on medium-high (80%) for about 10 seconds.

LITTLE STUFFED TOMATOES

The shape of plum tomatoes makes great "shells" to contain filling.

Firm small roma (plum) tomatoes	8	8
Salt	½ tsp.	2 mL
Tiny flower pasta (stellini)	⅔ cup	150 mL
Boiling water	4 cups	1 L
Salt	1 tsp.	5 mL
Non-fat spreadable herb and garlic-flavored cream cheese	¼ cup	60 mL
Non-fat sour cream	¼ cup	60 mL
Finely chopped English cucumber	½ cup	125 mL
Finely chopped green onion	1 tbsp.	15 mL
Finely chopped fresh sweet basil	2 tsp.	10 mL
Chopped fresh parsley	2 tsp.	10 mL
Salt	½ tsp.	2 mL
Freshly ground pepper, sprinkle		
Thin cucumber slices, for garnish		

Cut tomatoes in half lengthwise. Scoop out inner pulp, discarding juice and seeds. Measure ½ cup (125 mL) pulp, discarding any extra. Sprinkle insides of tomato halves with first amount of salt. Turn upside down on paper towel. Let stand for 30 minutes to drain. Blot insides of tomato halves with paper towel to dry well.

Cook pasta in boiling water and second amount of salt in medium saucepan for 6 to 7 minutes, stirring occasionally, until tender but firm. Drain. Rinse with cold water. Drain.

Combine cream cheese and sour cream in medium bowl until smooth.

Stir in pasta. Add reserved tomato flesh, cucumber, green onion, basil, parsley, third amount of salt and pepper. Mix well. Cover. Chill until tomatoes are ready to be filled. Spoon rounded tablespoonful of filling into each tomato half. Garnish with pieces of cucumber. Makes 16 stuffed tomatoes.

1 stuffed tomato: 32 Calories; 0.3 g Total Fat; 177 mg Sodium; 1 g Protein; 7 g Carbohydrate; 1 g Dietary Fiber

Pictured on page 18.

STUFFED EGGS

Eggs brighten an antipasto tray. These have a bit darker stuffing due to anchovy paste.

Hard-boiled eggs, peeled and halved lengthwise	8	8
Anchovy paste	1½ tsp.	7 mL
Olive oil	2 tbsp.	30 mL
Parsley flakes	¼ tsp.	1 mL
Garlic powder	⅛ tsp.	0.5 mL
Prepared mustard	¼ tsp.	1 mL
Salt	⅛ tsp.	0.5 mL
Pepper, light sprinkle		
Paprika, sprinkle		

Carefully remove egg yolks from whites. Mash yolks in small bowl with fork.

Add next 7 ingredients. Mash together. If too dry, add more olive oil. Fill egg whites. Sprinkle with paprika. Makes 16 stuffed eggs.

1 stuffed egg: 69 Calories; 5.8 g Total Fat; 114 mg Sodium; 3 g Protein; 1 g Carbohydrate; trace Dietary Fiber

Pictured on page 17.

APPETIZER CONES

A creamy yellow center. Preparation time is only 20 minutes.

Tiny bow pasta (farfallini)	⅔ cup	150 mL
Boiling water	4 cups	1 L
Salt	1 tsp.	5 mL
Green onion, finely chopped	1	1
Very finely chopped dill pickle, blotted dry	½ cup	125 mL
Finely chopped celery	2 tbsp.	30 mL
Non-fat spreadable cream cheese	⅓ cup	75 mL
Skim milk	1 tbsp.	15 mL
Prepared mustard	1 tsp.	5 mL
Salt	1 tsp.	5 mL
Granulated sugar	1 tsp.	5 mL
Celery seed	¼ tsp.	1 mL
Grated light Swiss cheese	½ cup	125 mL
Round non-fat ham slices (4 in., 10 cm, in diameter), cut in half	12	12

Cook pasta in boiling water and first amount of salt in medium saucepan for 5 to 6 minutes, stirring occasionally, until tender but firm. Drain. Rinse with cold water. Drain.

Place pasta in medium bowl. Add next 3 ingredients.

Combine next 6 ingredients in small bowl until smooth. Add to pasta mixture.

Add Swiss cheese. Mix well.

Shape ham slices into cone shapes. Secure with wooden picks. Place about 1 tbsp. (15 mL) pasta mixture inside each cone. Makes 24 cones.

1 stuffed cone: 47 Calories; 0.6 g Total Fat; 306 mg Sodium; 3 g Protein; 7 g Carbohydrate; trace Dietary Fiber

Pictured on page 17.

CREAMY LOX SHELLS

Lox is a type of smoked salmon that has been cured in brine and then cold-smoked. Slightly saltier than some other smoked salmons but can be used interchangeably.

Large (not jumbo) shell pasta (2½ oz., 70 g)	¾ cup	175 mL
Boiling water	4 cups	1 L
Salt	1 tsp.	5 mL
Light spreadable cream cheese	8 oz.	250 g
Light salad dressing (or mayonnaise)	1 tbsp.	15 mL
Lemon juice	½ tsp.	2 mL
Freshly ground pepper, sprinkle		
Finely chopped lox	⅓ cup	75 mL
Finely chopped fresh dill (or ½ tsp., 2 mL, dried)	2 tsp.	10 mL
Granulated sugar	⅛ tsp.	0.5 mL

Fresh dill sprigs, for garnish

Cook pasta in boiling water and salt in large saucepan for 8 to 10 minutes, stirring occasionally, until tender but firm. Drain. Rinse with cold water until cool. Drain. Let stand on paper towel until dry.

Beat cream cheese, salad dressing and lemon juice together in small bowl until smooth. Add pepper, lox, dill and sugar. Mix well.

Spoon about 1 tsp. (5 mL) filling into each shell. Garnish with dill. Cover. Chill until cold. Makes about 60 shells.

1 filled shell: 15 Calories; 0.8 g Total Fat; 72 mg Sodium; 1 g Protein; 1 g Carbohydrate; trace Dietary Fiber

Pictured on page 17.

What is antipasto?

Italian for "cold hors d'œuvres," the word antipasto originated from pasto (meal) and ante (before). It is a plate of appetizers which may include cured or smoked meat, cheeses, peppers, seafood salads, stuffed mushrooms, raw vegetables or marinated vegetables, artichoke hearts, olives, anchovies, sardines, bread sticks and more. Of course, in North America, we are more familiar with a more modern antipasto where everything is cut up in a sauce.

ANTIPASTO

Use some, freeze some—always be prepared.
Serve with party crackers or toast cups.

Finely chopped cauliflower	1 cup	250 mL
Finely chopped pitted ripe olives	½ cup	125 mL
Finely chopped pimiento-stuffed olives	¼ cup	60 mL
Chopped pickled onions	½ cup	125 mL
Cooking oil	¼ cup	60 mL
Can of mushroom pieces, drained and chopped	10 oz.	284 mL
Small green pepper, finely chopped	1	1
Ketchup	2¼ cups	550 mL
Jar of sweet mixed pickles, drained and juice reserved, finely chopped	12 oz.	341 mL
Finely chopped red pepper (optional)	¼ cup	60 mL
Reserved pickle juice	3 tbsp.	50 mL
Can of tuna, drained and flaked	6½ oz.	184 g
Can of broken (or cocktail) shrimp, drained and rinsed	4 oz.	113 g

Put first 5 ingredients into large saucepan. Bring to a boil on medium. Reduce heat. Simmer for 10 minutes.

Add next 6 ingredients. Bring to a boil. Reduce heat. Simmer, uncovered, for 10 minutes, stirring often.

Add tuna and shrimp. Stir. Chill. Makes 6 cups (1.5 L).

2 tbsp. (30 mL): 40 Calories; 1.6 g Total Fat; 244 mg Sodium; 2 g Protein; 5 g Carbohydrate; 1 g Dietary Fiber

Variation: Use dill pickles rather than sweet.

ANTIPASTO

A favorite Italian appetizer. This may be served in the living room before the meal or at the dining room table.

Prosciutto (or ham) slices	8	8
Genoa salami slices	8	8
Mortadella slices	8	8
Provolone (or other) cheese, cubed	8	8
Can of artichoke hearts, drained and quartered	14 oz.	398 mL
Pitted ripe olives	16	16
Pimiento-stuffed olives	16	16
Honeydew melon wedges	8	8
Cantaloupe wedges	8	8
Stuffed Eggs, page 10	16	16

Cut large meat slices. Roll up. Arrange on platter.

Arrange remaining 8 ingredients on platter. Serves 8.

1 serving: 446 Calories; 30.1 g Total Fat; 1577 mg Sodium; 24 g Protein; 22 g Carbohydrate; 3 g Dietary Fiber

Pictured on page 17.

Salads

ith the variety of vegetables and pasta used in Italian salads, you won't get tired of these recipes. Served warm or cold, there's a salad to start your meal or to eat as a main course. Try Creamy Shrimp Salad, this page, or Bruschetta In A Bowl, page 20, for something a bit different. For maximum variety, fix up Antipasto Salad, page 15, or Warm Pesto Salad, page 19.

CREAMY SHRIMP SALAD

Serve this salad in butter lettuce cups or hollowed-out tomato halves. Can also be served on a bed of crisp lettuce.

Tiny shell pasta	1 cup	250 mL
Boiling water	6 cups	1.5 L
Salt	1½ tsp.	7 mL
Ripe medium tomatoes, seeded and diced	3	3
Finely diced green pepper	½ cup	125 mL
Small cooked shrimp (fresh or frozen, thawed)	1 cup	250 mL
Green onions, thinly sliced	2	2
Non-fat salad dressing (or mayonnaise)	¼ cup	60 mL
Non-fat sour cream	¼ cup	60 mL
Seafood cocktail sauce	3 tbsp.	50 mL
Lemon juice	1 tbsp.	15 mL
Prepared horseradish	¼ tsp.	1 mL
Granulated sugar	⅛ tsp.	0.5 mL
Salt	⅛ tsp.	0.5 mL
Freshly ground pepper, sprinkle		

Cook pasta in boiling water and first amount of salt in large saucepan for 10 to 12 minutes, stirring occasionally, until tender but firm. Drain. Rinse with cold water. Drain. Place in medium bowl.

Add tomato, green pepper, shrimp and green onion. Toss.

Mix remaining 8 ingredients in small bowl. Pour over pasta mixture. Mix well. Makes 6 cups (1.5 L).

1 cup (250 mL): 125 Calories; 0.8 g Total Fat; 294 mg Sodium; 8 g Protein; 21 g Carbohydrate; 1 g Dietary Fiber

Pictured on page 18.

STUFFED TOMATO SALAD

A genuine summer salad when you use vine-ripened tomatoes.

Medium tomatoes, hollowed out and flesh reserved	6	6
Salt	1 tsp.	5 mL
Orzo pasta	½ cup	125 mL
Boiling water	4 cups	1 L
Salt	1 tsp.	5 mL
Dry white (or alcohol-free) wine	¼ cup	60 mL
Balsamic vinegar	1 tsp.	5 mL
Reserved tomato flesh, chopped	1 cup	250 mL
Basil Pesto, page 91	1 tsp.	5 mL
Pectin granules	½ tsp.	2 mL
Freshly ground pepper, sprinkle		
Green onion, sliced	1	1
Diced green, red, orange or yellow pepper	¼ cup	60 mL
Thinly shredded radicchio	¼ cup	60 mL
Grated carrot	¼ cup	60 mL

Sprinkle insides of tomatoes with first amount of salt. Turn upside down on paper towel to drain. Blot insides with paper towel to dry.

Cook pasta in boiling water and second amount of salt in medium saucepan for 8 to 10 minutes, stirring occasionally, until tender but firm. Drain. Rinse with cold water. Drain. Place in medium bowl.

Combine next 6 ingredients in jar. Cover. Shake until well mixed. Pour over pasta.

Stir in remaining 4 ingredients. Toss well. Stuff each tomato with salad. Makes 6 stuffed tomatoes.

1 stuffed tomato: 119 Calories; 1.3 g Total Fat; 471 mg Sodium; 4 g Protein; 22 g Carbohydrate; 2 g Dietary Fiber

VEGETABLE PASTA SALAD

Brightened with red and green strips of pepper and zucchini. Has a lively taste as well.

Rotini pasta (about 8 oz., 225 g)	3 cups	750 mL
Boiling water	10 cups	2.5 L
Cooking oil (optional)	1 tbsp.	15 mL
Salt	2 tsp.	10 mL
Medium red pepper, slivered	1	1
Slivered zucchini, with peel	2 cups	500 mL
Sliced green onion	¼ cup	60 mL
Medium fresh mushrooms, sliced	6	6
Sliced celery	½ cup	125 mL
Cooking oil	⅓ cup	75 mL
Red wine vinegar	¼ cup	60 mL
Grated Parmesan cheese	2 tbsp.	30 mL
Salt	1 tsp.	5 mL
Pepper	¼ tsp.	1 mL
Dried whole oregano	¼ tsp.	1 mL
Dried sweet basil	¼ tsp.	1 mL
Garlic powder	¼ tsp.	1 mL

Cook pasta in boiling water, cooking oil and first amount of salt in large uncovered pot or Dutch oven for 10 to 12 minutes, stirring occasionally, until tender but firm. Drain. Rinse with cold water. Drain. Return to pot.

Add next 5 ingredients. Stir.

Mix remaining 8 ingredients in small bowl. Pour over pasta mixture. Stir to coat well. Makes about 8 cups (2 L).

1 cup (250 mL): 223 Calories; 10.7 g Total Fat; 380 mg Sodium; 6 g Protein; 27 g Carbohydrate; 2 g Dietary Fiber

Pictured on front cover.

ANTIPASTO SALAD

Serve as the first course or as a main course accompaniment. Great with any barbecue meal.

ITALIAN DRESSING

Condensed chicken broth	1 cup	250 mL
Cornstarch	2 tsp.	10 mL
White wine vinegar	¾ cup	175 mL
Dried sweet basil	2 tsp.	10 mL
Dried whole oregano	2 tsp.	10 mL
Garlic cloves, crushed	2	2
Granulated sugar	1 tsp.	5 mL
Broccoli florets	2 cups	500 mL
Small red onion, thinly sliced	1	1
Medium green pepper, cut into ¼ inch (6 mm) slices	1	1
Medium red pepper, cut into ¼ inch (6 mm) slices	1	1
Medium yellow pepper, cut into ¼ inch (6 mm) slices	1	1
Can of artichoke hearts, drained and quartered	14 oz.	398 mL
Can of chick peas (garbanzo beans), drained	19 oz.	540 mL
Can of flaked white tuna, packed in water, drained	6½ oz.	184 g

Italian Dressing: Combine first 7 ingredients in medium saucepan. Bring to a boil, stirring until slightly thickened. Stir in broccoli florets. Remove from heat. Cool to room temperature.

Combine remaining 7 ingredients in large bowl. Add dressing. Toss well. Chill for several hours or overnight, stirring occasionally. Just before serving, stir salad and drain off dressing. Makes 10 cups (2.5 L).

1 cup (250 mL): 99 Calories; 1.3 g Total Fat; 277 mg Sodium; 8 g Protein; 15 g Carbohydrate; 3 g Dietary Fiber

Pictured on page 18.

Variation: Substitute any of the vegetables with thinly sliced zucchini, sliced fresh mushrooms, whole pitted ripe olives or tomato wedges.

TOMATO CHEESE SALAD

Attractive as well as easy.

Medium tomatoes, seeded and cut bite size	8	8
Mozzarella cheese, diced	8 oz.	225 g
Pitted ripe olives	16-24	16-24
Dried sweet basil	½ tsp.	2 mL
Olive oil	¼ cup	60 mL
Salt, sprinkle		
Pepper, sprinkle		
Lettuce leaves	3-4	3-4

Combine tomato, cheese, olives and basil in medium bowl. Stir.

Add olive oil. Toss. Sprinkle with salt and pepper. Toss.

Line large plate with lettuce leaves. Arrange salad on top. Makes 4 cups (1 L).

½ cup (125 mL): 200 Calories; 16.3 g Total Fat; 218 mg Sodium; 8 g Protein; 7 g Carbohydrate; 2 g Dietary Fiber

To reduce the acidity of tomatoes in a recipe, add ½ tsp. (2 mL) sugar for each 14 oz. (398 mL) can of tomatoes.

ARTICHOKE SALAD

To save time, cook pasta while preparing vegetables. Tomato wedges and pine nuts make a nice garnish.

TOMATO VINAIGRETTE

Tomato juice	1 cup	250 mL
White wine vinegar	3 tbsp.	50 mL
Basil Pesto, page 91	1 tbsp.	15 mL
Pectin granules	1 tbsp.	15 mL
Granulated sugar	½ tsp.	2 mL

SALAD

Rotini pasta (about 4 oz., 113 g)	1½ cups	375 mL
Fresh (or frozen or dried) cheese-filled tortellini	4 oz.	113 g
Boiling water	12 cups	3 L
Salt	1 tbsp.	15 mL
Can of artichoke hearts, drained and quartered	14 oz.	398 mL
Chopped pitted ripe olives	2 tbsp.	30 mL
Medium red pepper, finely chopped	½	½
Medium red onion, finely chopped	½	½
Medium carrot, grated	1	1
Grated light Parmesan cheese	1 tbsp.	15 mL

Tomato Vinaigrette: Combine all 5 ingredients in jar. Cover. Shake well. Let stand at room temperature for 20 minutes until slightly thickened. Makes about 1¼ cups (300 mL) vinaigrette.

Salad: Cook both pastas in boiling water and salt in large uncovered pot or Dutch oven for 10 minutes, stirring occasionally, until tender but firm. Drain. Rinse with cold water. Drain.

Combine next 6 ingredients in large bowl. Add vinaigrette and pasta. Toss well. Makes 7 cups (1.75 L).

1 cup (250 mL): 150 Calories; 3.3 g Total Fat; 315 mg Sodium; 6 g Protein; 25 g Carbohydrate; 3 g Dietary Fiber

1. Antipasto, page 12
2. Creamy Lox Shells, page 11
3. Stuffed Eggs, page 10
4. Appetizer Cones, page 11
5. Fried Mozzarella, page 9

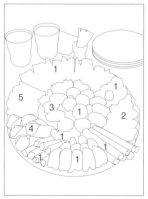

Props Courtesy Of: Winners Stores

WARM PESTO SALAD

This salad takes a little more time but is well worth the effort. Can be served as a main course.

Olive oil	½ cup	125 mL
Large garlic cloves, coarsely chopped	5	5
Coarsely chopped fresh sweet basil	½ cup	125 mL
Chopped fresh parsley	¼ cup	60 mL
Freshly ground pepper, sprinkle		
Medium Japanese eggplant, cut lengthwise into slices about ¼ inch (6 mm) thick	1	1
Cob of corn, husked	1	1
Small red (or Spanish) onion, cut into thick slices	1	1
Small red pepper, halved	1	1
Small yellow pepper, halved	1	1
Large head of radicchio, quartered	1	1
Top sirloin steak (1 inch, 2.5 cm, thick), trimmed of fat	¾ lb.	340 g
Mixed greens, torn bite size	6 cups	1.5 L
Roma (plum) tomatoes, diced	2	2
Grated Parmesan cheese	2 tbsp.	30 mL

Preheat barbecue to high. Process first 5 ingredients in blender, scraping down sides as needed, until smooth. Makes ⅔ cup (150 mL) basting sauce.

Brush sauce heavily on eggplant.

Brush remaining sauce lightly on corn, red onion, peppers, radicchio and steak. Sear steak on greased grill for 1 minute per side. Cook for 3 to 4 minutes per side until desired doneness. Reduce heat to medium. Remove steak to cutting board. Place vegetables on greased grill. Close lid. Cook for about 10 minutes, turning occasionally, until tender-crisp and corn kernels are starting to pop. As vegetables are cooked, remove to cutting board and cut bite size. Cut corn off cob. Place all vegetables in large bowl. Slice steak very thinly across grain. Add to vegetables.

Add mixed greens. Toss together well. Add tomato and cheese. Makes about 12 cups (3 L).

2 cups (500 mL): 326 Calories; 22.6 g Total Fat; 96 mg Sodium; 16 g Protein; 18 g Carbohydrate; 5 g Dietary Fiber

1. Antipasto Salad, page 15
2. Creamy Shrimp Salad, page 13
3. Little Stuffed Tomatoes, page 10

Props Courtesy Of: The Bay

BRUSCHETTA IN A BOWL

Day-old bread is used to decrease the absorption of the liquid in the salad and for ease of cubing.

Cubed day-old Italian bread	4 cups	1 L
Balsamic vinegar	⅓ cup	75 mL
English cucumber, quartered lengthwise and sliced	1	1
Medium red or yellow pepper, chopped	1	1
Roma (plum) tomatoes, diced	3	3
Freshly ground pepper	¼ tsp.	1 mL
Finely chopped fresh sweet basil	¼ cup	60 mL
Sliced pitted ripe olives	¼ cup	60 mL
Olive oil	2 tsp.	10 mL

Spread bread cubes on large ungreased baking sheet. Bake in 350°F (175°C) oven for 5 minutes. Stir. Bake for 10 to 15 minutes until toasted.

Combine remaining 8 ingredients in medium bowl. Add bread cubes. Toss. Makes 7 cups (1.75 L).

1 cup (250 mL): 109 Calories; 2.1 g Total Fat; 184 mg Sodium; 3 g Protein; 20 g Carbohydrate; 2 g Dietary Fiber

ARTICHOKE SALAD

Delicate-looking with an unusual combination of ingredients.

Assorted lettuce leaves	24	24
Radicchio leaves	8	8
Endive leaves	8	8
Containers of alfalfa sprouts (5 oz., 135 g, each)	2	2
Cans of artichoke hearts (14 oz., 398 mL, each), drained and quartered	2	2
Diced green pepper	2 tbsp.	30 mL
Diced red pepper	2 tbsp.	30 mL
Diced yellow pepper	2 tbsp.	30 mL
Hard-boiled eggs, sliced	3	3

Creamy Italian (or creamy vinaigrette) dressing

Divide salad greens among 6 individual salad plates.

Divide alfalfa sprouts over greens. Spread evenly. Spoon artichoke pieces over sprouts. Sprinkle with diced peppers. Arrange about 2 egg slices alongside salad.

Drizzle with dressing. Serves 6.

1 serving: 194 Calories; 13.5 g Total Fat; 510 mg Sodium; 8 g Protein; 13 g Carbohydrate; 6 g Dietary Fiber

Artichokes turn black due to the natural enzymes they contain. Cooking artichokes thoroughly will prevent the color change.

PROSCIUTTO AND MELON SALAD

Prosciutto (proh-SHOO-toh) is the Italian word for ham that has been seasoned, salt-cured and air-dried.

Tubetti pasta	1⅓ cups	325 mL
Boiling water	6 cups	1.5 L
Salt	1½ tsp.	7 mL
Lean prosciutto (or ham), trimmed of fat and finely chopped	3 oz.	85 g
Diced cantaloupe	2 cups	500 mL
Finely chopped red onion	¼ cup	60 mL
Chopped fresh parsley	¼ cup	60 mL
Non-fat sour cream	½ cup	125 mL
Skim evaporated milk	⅓ cup	75 mL
Liquid honey	2 tbsp.	30 mL
Dijon mustard	1 tbsp.	15 mL
Finely grated lemon peel	¾ tsp.	4 mL
Salt	⅛ tsp.	0.5 mL

Freshly ground pepper, sprinkle

Cook pasta in boiling water and first amount of salt in medium saucepan for about 8 minutes, stirring occasionally, until tender but firm. Drain. Rinse with cold water. Drain. Place in medium bowl.

Add prosciutto, cantaloupe, red onion and parsley.

Combine next 6 ingredients in small bowl. Whisk until smooth. Pour over pasta mixture. Mix well.

Sprinkle with pepper. Chill. Makes 5 cups (1.25 L).

1 cup (250 mL): 223 Calories; 3.2 g Total Fat; 631 mg Sodium; 13 g Protein; 36 g Carbohydrate; 1 g Dietary Fiber

TOMATO PASTA SALAD

Preparation time is 30 minutes. Other pasta can be substituted for the bow pasta.

Medium bow pasta (about 10 oz., 285 g)	4 cups	1 L
Boiling water	4 cups	1 L
Salt	1 tsp.	5 mL
Medium roma (plum) tomatoes, diced	6	6
Chopped fresh sweet basil, packed	½ cup	125 mL
Part-skim mozzarella cheese, cut into very small cubes	4 oz.	113 g
Sliced pitted ripe olives (optional)	¼ cup	60 mL
TOMATO DRESSING		
Tomato juice	½ cup	125 mL
Red wine vinegar	2 tbsp.	30 mL
Olive oil	1 tbsp.	15 mL
Garlic cloves, minced	2	2
Worcestershire sauce	½ tsp.	2 mL
Salt	½ tsp.	2 mL
Freshly ground pepper	⅛ tsp.	0.5 mL

Cook pasta in boiling water and salt in large saucepan for about 6 minutes, stirring occasionally, until tender but firm. Drain. Rinse with cold water. Drain.

Combine tomato, basil, cheese, olives and pasta in large bowl.

Tomato Dressing: Combine all 7 ingredients in jar. Cover. Shake. Pour over salad. Toss well. Let stand at room temperature for at least 30 minutes to allow flavors to blend. Makes 12 cups (3 L).

1 cup (250 mL): 147 Calories; 3.5 g Total Fat; 211 mg Sodium; 7 g Protein; 23 g Carbohydrate; 1 g Dietary Fiber

PASTA BEAN SALAD

The perfect salad to take on a picnic.

BALSAMIC DRESSING

Non-fat Italian dressing	½ cup	125 mL
Reserved juice from tomatoes		
Grated light Parmesan cheese	2 tbsp.	30 mL
Balsamic vinegar	1 tbsp.	15 mL
Garlic clove, minced	1	1
Granulated sugar	1 tsp.	5 mL
Dried sweet basil, just a pinch		
Dried thyme, just a pinch		
Elbow macaroni (about 8 oz., 225 g)	2 cups	500 mL
Boiling water	8 cups	2 L
Salt	2 tsp.	10 mL
Can of mixed beans, drained and rinsed	19 oz.	540 mL
Medium red onion, thinly sliced	½	½
Medium green, red, orange or yellow pepper, thinly sliced into 2 inch (5 cm) lengths	½	½
Medium carrot, coarsely grated	1	1
Can of stewed tomatoes, drained and juice reserved, chopped	14 oz.	398 mL

Balsamic Dressing: Combine all 8 ingredients in jar. Cover. Shake well. Let stand for 15 minutes to allow flavors to blend. Makes 1⅓ cups (325 mL) dressing.

Cook macaroni in boiling water and salt in large saucepan for about 8 minutes, stirring occasionally, until tender but firm. Do not overcook. Drain. Rinse with cold water. Drain. Place in large bowl.

Add remaining 5 ingredients. Pour dressing over pasta mixture. Mix well. Serve immediately or cover and chill. Makes 8 cups (2 L).

1 cup (250 mL): 178 Calories; 1.1 g Total Fat; 421 mg Sodium; 7 g Protein; 35 g Carbohydrate; 4 g Dietary Fiber

To check if the casserole you are baking is heated through, insert a knife in the center and hold it there for 10 seconds. Remove the knife and touch the tip with your fingers. If the knife is warm or hot, the casserole is ready.

Soups

bit of broth, some veggies and a meat make a wonderful warm brew for your insides. Italian takes that a step further with several versions of minestrone, pages 24 and 25. Beans also make a nutritious and flavorful addition to soup in Zuppa Fagioli and Fagioli Soup, both page 28.

GARBANZO SOUP

This has its own good flavor. Great choice.

Cooking oil	2 tbsp.	30 mL
Chopped onion	1½ cups	375 mL
Can of diced tomatoes, with juice	14 oz.	398 mL
Ketchup	2 tbsp.	30 mL
Instant vegetable stock mix	2 tbsp.	30 mL
Dried whole oregano	1 tsp.	5 mL
Garlic powder	¼ tsp.	1 mL
Salt	½ tsp.	2 mL
Pepper	⅛ tsp.	0.5 mL
Cayenne pepper	⅛ tsp.	0.5 mL
Water	3 cups	750 mL
Can of garbanzo beans (chick peas), with liquid	19 oz.	540 mL
Plain yogurt (or sour cream)	6 tbsp.	100 mL

Heat cooking oil in large saucepan. Add onion. Sauté until onion is soft.

Add next 9 ingredients. Bring to a boil, stirring often. Boil gently for 15 minutes.

Process garbanzo beans in blender until smooth. Add to tomato mixture. Stir. Return to a boil. Boil gently for about 10 minutes to allow flavors to blend.

Add 1 tbsp. (15 mL) yogurt to center of each individual serving. Makes 6 cups (1.5 L).

1 cup (250 mL): 204 Calories; 7.8 g Total Fat; 660 mg Sodium; 7 g Protein; 28 g Carbohydrate; 4 g Dietary Fiber

Minestrone

This hearty thick soup usually contains pasta and peas or beans. Serve with grated Parmesan or Romano cheese on top. The word minestrone comes from the Italian word minestra, a medium thick soup which may have meat and vegetables as ingredients. Minestrina is a thin broth.

ITALIAN MINESTRONE

Rich red broth with lots of vegetables and pasta. Very satisfying. Takes only 15 minutes to chop vegetables. Makes enough to feed a crowd.

Chopped onion	1 cup	250 mL
Garlic cloves, minced	2	2
Olive oil	2 tsp.	10 mL
Chopped celery, with some leaves	1 cup	250 mL
Water	8 cups	2 L
Can of diced tomatoes, with juice	28 oz.	796 mL
Vegetable bouillon powder	1 tbsp.	15 mL
Parsley flakes	1 tbsp.	15 mL
Crushed dried thyme	1 tsp.	5 mL
Chili powder	½ tsp.	2 mL
Salt	½ tsp.	2 mL
Ground rosemary	⅛ tsp.	0.5 mL
Bay leaf	1	1
Cayenne pepper, pinch		
Diced carrot	2 cups	500 mL
Diced zucchini, with peel	1½ cups	375 mL
Finely chopped cabbage	1 cup	250 mL
Can of white kidney beans, drained and rinsed	14 oz.	398 mL
Cans of red kidney beans (14 oz., 398 mL, each), with liquid	2	2
Elbow macaroni (about 4 oz., 113 g)	1 cup	250 mL
Boiling water	6 cups	1.5 L
Salt	1½ tsp.	7 mL
Freshly grated Parmesan cheese, sprinkle (optional)		

Sauté onion and garlic in olive oil in large uncovered pot or Dutch oven for 1 minute. Add celery. Sauté for 3 to 4 minutes until onion is soft.

Add next 13 ingredients. Bring to a boil. Reduce heat. Simmer, partially covered, for 40 minutes until carrot is tender.

Mash about ½ can of white kidney beans with fork. Stir into soup. Add remaining white kidney beans, and red kidney beans with liquid. Simmer, partially covered, for 20 minutes.

Cook macaroni in boiling water and second amount of salt in large saucepan for 7 to 8 minutes, stirring occasionally, until tender but firm. Drain well. Add to soup. Sprinkle individual servings with Parmesan cheese. Makes 17 cups (4.25 L).

1 cup (250 mL): 115 Calories; 1.2 g Total Fat; 484 mg Sodium; 6 g Protein; 21 g Carbohydrate; 5 g Dietary Fiber

Pictured on page 35.

SPEEDY MINESTRONE

By using canned beans, preparation time has been reduced. A full meal.

Bacon slices, cut into small pieces	4	4
Large onion, chopped	1	1
Lean ground beef	1½ lbs.	680 g
Boiling water	6 cups	1.5 L
Beef bouillon cubes (⅕ oz., 6 g, each)	6	6
Canned spaghetti sauce	2 cups	500 mL
Chopped cabbage	2 cups	500 mL
Celery rib, chopped	1	1
Medium carrot, diced	1	1
Sliced zucchini	1 cup	250 mL
Salt	1 tsp.	5 mL
Pepper	¼ tsp.	1 mL
Garlic powder	¼ tsp.	1 mL
Can of red kidney beans, with liquid	14 oz.	398 mL
Broken vermicelli pasta, uncooked	½ cup	125 mL

Put bacon, onion and ground beef into large pot. Sauté until bacon is cooked, onion is soft and no pink remains in beef. Drain.

Combine water and bouillon cubes. Stir to dissolve. Add to beef mixture.

Add next 8 ingredients. Bring to a boil. Reduce heat. Cover. Simmer for 30 minutes.

Add beans with liquid and pasta. Simmer, stirring occasionally, for 10 minutes. Makes about 12 cups (3 L).

1 cup (250 mL): 274 Calories; 16.8 g Total Fat; 1396 mg Sodium; 15 g Protein; 16 g Carbohydrate; 4 g Dietary Fiber

MINESTRONE

Perfect for a cold winter evening. Serve with salad and buns.

Cooking oil	2 tbsp.	30 mL
Lean ground beef	1 lb.	454 g
Chopped onion	1½ cups	375 mL
Chopped celery	1 cup	250 mL
Boiling water	6 cups	1.5 L
Beef bouillon powder	3 tbsp.	50 mL
Cans of diced tomatoes, (14 oz., 398 mL, each), with juice	3	3
Grated cabbage, packed	2 cups	500 mL
Thinly sliced carrot	¾ cup	175 mL
Parsley flakes	1 tbsp.	15 mL
Salt	1 tsp.	5 mL
Pepper	¼ tsp.	1 mL
Garlic powder	¼ tsp.	1 mL
Elbow macaroni (about 4 oz., 113 g), uncooked	1 cup	250 mL
Can of red kidney beans, with liquid	14 oz.	398 mL

Grated Parmesan cheese

Heat cooking oil in frying pan. Scramble-fry ground beef, onion and celery until no pink remains in beef and onion and celery are soft. Drain. Put into large pot or Dutch oven.

Mix boiling water and bouillon powder. Add to pot.

Add next 7 ingredients. Bring to a boil, stirring occasionally. Boil gently for 15 minutes.

Stir in macaroni. Return to a boil. Boil gently for 10 minutes.

Add kidney beans with liquid. Stir. Boil for about 5 minutes until macaroni is tender.

Sprinkle individual servings with Parmesan cheese. Makes 12 cups (3 L).

1 cup (250 mL): 208 Calories; 8.8 g Total Fat; 1002 mg Sodium; 12 g Protein; 21 g Carbohydrate; 4 g Dietary Fiber

TORTELLINI SOUP

A broth-type soup with pasta that is different, good, and freezes well.

Water	6 cups	1.5 L
Chopped onion	1 cup	250 mL
Chopped celery	½ cup	125 mL
Sliced carrot	½ cup	125 mL
Chicken bouillon powder	2 tbsp.	30 mL
Parsley flakes	1 tsp.	5 mL
Salt	½ tsp.	2 mL
Pepper	⅛ tsp.	0.5 mL
Dried rosemary	⅛ tsp.	0.5 mL

FILLING		
Finely chopped cooked chicken	½ cup	125 mL
Grated Parmesan cheese	1 tbsp.	15 mL
Water		

TORTELLINI		
All-purpose flour	1 cup	250 mL
Large eggs	2	2
Salt	¼ tsp.	1 mL
Sliced fresh mushrooms	¼ cup	60 mL

Put first 9 ingredients into large saucepan. Bring to a boil. Reduce heat. Cover. Simmer for 20 minutes.

Filling: Combine chicken and Parmesan cheese, adding just enough water to hold mixture together.

Tortellini: Mix first 3 ingredients to form stiff dough. Divide in half. Roll out 1 portion on lightly floured surface until very thin. Cut into twelve 2 inch (5 cm) circles. Put ¼ tsp. (1 mL) filling on each. Moisten edge with water. Fold over. Press to seal. Pull ends together away from curved side. Moisten edges with water to seal. Repeat with remaining dough and filling. Place pasta on floured tray. Cover with damp tea towel until ready to cook. Makes 24 tortellini.

Add mushrooms and tortellini to saucepan. Return to a boil. Reduce heat. Cover. Simmer for 15 minutes until tortellini is tender but firm. Makes about 5½ cups (1.4 L).

1 cup (250 mL): 179 Calories; 3.8 g Total Fat; 1032 mg Sodium; 14 g Protein; 22 g Carbohydrate; 2 g Dietary Fiber

TORTELLINI IN BROTH

Homemade tortellini makes this soup exceptional, but if time is short, commercial tortellini is also good! Very quick and easy to prepare.

Cans of condensed chicken broth (10 oz., 284 mL, each)	3	3
Water	3½ cups	875 mL
Broccoli florets	2 cups	500 mL
Green onions, thinly sliced	4	4
Mushroom-Filled Tortellini, page 48 (½ of recipe), or 1 lb., 454 g, commercial cheese or meat-filled tortellini (see Note)	50	50

Grated light Parmesan cheese, sprinkle (optional)

Bring chicken broth and water to a boil in large uncovered pot or Dutch oven. Add broccoli and green onion. Reduce heat. Simmer, partially covered, for 4 to 5 minutes.

Add tortellini. Bring to a boil. Reduce heat. Simmer, partially covered, for 4 to 5 minutes until tortellini is tender but firm.

Sprinkle Parmesan cheese over individual servings. Makes 9 cups (2.25 L).

1 cup (250 mL): 144 Calories; 2 g Total Fat; 913 mg Sodium; 10 g Protein; 22 g Carbohydrate; 1 g Dietary Fiber

Note: If using commercial tortellini, add to soup at same time as broccoli and green onion. Cook for 10 to 12 minutes until tortellini is tender but firm.

LENTIL AND PASTA SOUP

A robust, hearty soup with lots of texture. About 20 minutes preparation time.

Garlic cloves, minced	2	2
Finely chopped onion	1 cup	250 mL
Chopped celery	1 cup	250 mL
Olive oil	2 tsp.	10 mL
Water	7 cups	1.75 L
Beef (or chicken) bouillon powder	2 tbsp.	30 mL
Can of tomatoes, with juice, processed	14 oz.	398 mL
Thinly sliced carrot	1½ cups	375 mL
Green lentils	¾ cup	175 mL
Parsley flakes	2 tsp.	10 mL
Dried sweet basil	1 tsp.	5 mL
Ground oregano, just a pinch		
Salt	1 tsp.	5 mL
Pepper, sprinkle		
Tubetti pasta, uncooked	1 cup	250 mL

Sauté garlic, onion and celery in olive oil in large uncovered pot or Dutch oven until onion is soft.

Add next 10 ingredients. Bring to a boil. Reduce heat. Simmer, partially covered, for 30 minutes.

Stir in pasta. Simmer for 15 minutes, stirring occasionally. Makes 8 cups (2 L).

1 cup (250 mL): 158 Calories; 2 g Total Fat; 893 mg Sodium; 8 g Protein; 28 g Carbohydrate; 4 g Dietary Fiber

Pictured on page 35.

Pick zucchinis that are 6 to 8 inches (15 cm to 21 cm) long for the best flavor.

SHELLED ZUCCHINI SOUP

This colorful soup has great flavor.

Mild Italian sausage, sliced ¼ inch (6 mm) thick	8 oz.	225 g
Chopped onion	1 cup	250 mL
Cans of condensed chicken consommé (10 oz., 284 mL, each)	2	2
Water	3 cups	750 mL
Garlic cloves, minced	1-2	1-2
Coarsely grated zucchini, with peel	4 cups	1 L
Grated carrot	1 cup	250 mL
Italian seasoning	1 tsp.	5 mL
Dried sweet basil	½ tsp.	2 mL
Dried whole oregano	½ tsp.	2 mL
Granulated sugar	½ tsp.	2 mL
Tiny shell pasta, uncooked	1 cup	250 mL

Grated mozzarella cheese (optional)

Sauté sausage and onion in large uncovered pot or Dutch oven until no pink remains in sausage.

Add next 9 ingredients. Stir. Bring to a boil. Reduce heat. Cover. Simmer gently for at least 30 minutes.

Add pasta. Simmer, stirring occasionally, until pasta is tender. If too thick, add more water.

Pour soup into individual broiler-proof bowls. Sprinkle with mozzarella cheese. Heat under broiler until browned. Makes 8 cups (2 L).

1 cup (250 mL): 204 Calories; 11 g Total Fat; 757 mg Sodium; 11 g Protein; 16 g Carbohydrate; 2 g Dietary Fiber

Pictured on page 35.

ZUPPA FAGIOLI

Fagioli (fawj-OH-lee) is the Italian word for "beans." A hearty Italian meal-in-one bean soup. Only 20 minutes preparation time.

Olive oil	1 tsp.	5 mL
Extra lean ground beef	½ lb.	225 g
Chopped onion	1 cup	250 mL
Chopped white celery heart (use inside ribs with leaves)	1 cup	250 mL
Medium carrot, grated	1	1
Garlic clove, minced	1	1
Can of roma (plum) tomatoes, with juice, puréed	28 oz.	796 mL
Can of white kidney beans, with liquid	19 oz.	540 mL
Can of beans in tomato sauce	14 oz.	398 mL
Liquid beef bouillon concentrate	2 tsp.	10 mL
Tomato paste	2 tbsp.	30 mL
Dried sweet basil	2 tsp.	10 mL
Dried whole oregano	¼ tsp.	1 mL
Dried thyme	¼ tsp.	1 mL
Dried crushed chilies	¼ tsp.	1 mL
Salt	½ tsp.	2 mL
Pepper	⅛ tsp.	0.5 mL
Granulated sugar	½ tsp.	2 mL
Water	3 cups	750 mL
Tubetti pasta, uncooked	1 cup	250 mL

Freshly ground pepper, sprinkle

Heat olive oil in large uncovered pot or Dutch oven. Scramble-fry ground beef, onion, celery, carrot and garlic until beef is no longer pink and vegetables are tender-crisp. Drain.

Add next 12 ingredients. Stir well.

Add water. Cover. Bring to a boil. Reduce heat. Simmer for 1 hour.

Stir in pasta. Simmer for 10 to 15 minutes, stirring occasionally, until pasta is tender but firm.

Sprinkle pepper over individual servings. Makes 12 cups (3 L).

1 cup (250 mL): 180 Calories; 3.8 g Total Fat; 660 mg Sodium; 11 g Protein; 27 g Carbohydrate; 7 g Dietary Fiber

FAGIOLI SOUP

Fawj-OH-lee soup has lots of beans and pasta. Broth is fairly thin.

Dried navy (white) beans	1 cup	250 mL
Water	8 cups	2 L
Ketchup	1 tbsp.	15 mL
Salt	1 tbsp.	15 mL
Pepper	¼ tsp.	1 mL
Garlic powder	½ tsp.	2 mL
Dried whole oregano	¼ tsp.	1 mL
Dried sweet basil	¼ tsp.	1 mL
Bay leaf	1	1
Tiny shell pasta, uncooked	1 cup	250 mL

Combine first 9 ingredients in large saucepan. Bring to a boil. Reduce heat. Cover. Simmer for 1½ to 2 hours until beans are tender. Discard bay leaf.

Add pasta. Simmer, stirring occasionally, for about 10 minutes until pasta is tender. If too thick, add water. Makes about 6½ cups (1.6 L).

1 cup (250 mL): 168 Calories; 0.7 g Total Fat; 1111 mg Sodium; 9 g Protein; 32 g Carbohydrate; 3 g Dietary Fiber

---

Big batches of soup are wonderful for freezing. Pour soup into containers that accommodate your family's needs and freeze. After the soup is frozen, turn out of the container and store in large freezer bags. Remember to label the bag for easy identification.

Brunch & Lunch

outhwatering mid-day fare can be easily prepared whether hot or cold dishes are your preference. Ham and Egg Fritatta, page 32, with Polenta Wedges, page 33, will give anyone a good start to the day. Edam cheese and basil are featured in Margherita Pizza, page 38, and Italian Focaccia Sandwiches, page 41, have the full flavor of sun-dried tomato pesto.

ZUCCHINI FRITTATA

Zucchini fits perfectly into this tasty concoction.

Cooking oil	1 tbsp.	15 mL
Medium onion, chopped	1	1
Medium potato, diced small	1	1
Medium zucchini, with peel, thinly sliced	2	2
Large eggs	8	8
Grated Parmesan cheese	2½ tbsp.	37 mL
Salt	½ tsp.	2 mL
Dried sweet basil, sprinkle		
Dried whole oregano, sprinkle		
Pepper, sprinkle		
Grated medium Cheddar cheese	½ cup	125 mL

Heat cooking oil in large non-stick frying pan. Add onion, potato and zucchini. Sauté until potato is almost cooked and onion and zucchini are soft.

Beat eggs in medium bowl until smooth. Add next 5 ingredients. Beat together well. Pour over zucchini mixture. Cover. Cook on medium-low for 13 to 15 minutes until eggs are set.

Remove from heat. Sprinkle with Cheddar cheese. Cover. Let stand for 2 to 4 minutes until cheese is melted. Serves 4.

1 serving: 299 Calories; 19.6 g Total Fat; 622 mg Sodium; 19 g Protein; 12 g Carbohydrate; 2 g Dietary Fiber

QUICK FRITTATA

Warming the hash browns cuts the baking time.
Meat and potatoes in this one.

Cooking oil	1 tbsp.	15 mL
Chopped onion	1 cup	250 mL
Bacon slices, cooked crisp and crumbled	6	6
Diced cooked ham (or 1 can ham flakes, 6½ oz., 184 g, drained)	¾ cup	175 mL
Frozen hash brown potatoes, warmed	3 cups	750 mL
Large eggs, fork-beaten	9	9
Water	3 tbsp.	50 mL
Paprika	1 tsp.	5 mL
Parsley flakes	1 tsp.	5 mL
Garlic powder	¼ tsp.	1 mL
Salt	¾ tsp.	4 mL
Pepper	¼ tsp.	1 mL

Heat cooking oil in frying pan. Add onion. Sauté until soft. Turn into greased 3 quart (3 L) casserole.

Add bacon, ham and potatoes. Stir.

Beat remaining 7 ingredients together in bowl until smooth. Pour over top. Bake, uncovered, in 400°F (205°C) oven for about 45 minutes until set. Cuts into 6 wedges.

1 wedge: 303 Calories; 5.2 g Total Fat; 824 mg Sodium; 18 g Protein; 24 g Carbohydrate; 3 g Dietary Fiber

---

Sweet bell peppers become even sweeter when cooked. However, be sure not to overcook, since this will cause the peppers to lose flavor, color and nutrients.

RED-TOPPED FRITTATA

Tomatoes nesting in a poofy egg pie. Serve at your next brunch.

Margarine (or butter)	2 tsp.	10 mL
Chopped onion	½ cup	125 mL
Diced green, red or yellow pepper	⅓ cup	75 mL
Chopped cooked ham (5 oz., 140 g)	1 cup	250 mL
Grated Edam (or Gouda) cheese	½ cup	125 mL
Large eggs, fork-beaten	6	6
Salt	1 tsp.	5 mL
Pepper, sprinkle		
Cayenne pepper, sprinkle		
Medium tomatoes, sliced	2	2

Melt margarine in large frying pan. Add onion. Sauté until onion is beginning to soften.

Add green pepper and ham. Sauté for 2 to 3 minutes. Turn into greased 10 inch (25 cm) glass pie plate or shallow 9 × 9 inch (22 × 22 cm) casserole.

Sprinkle with cheese.

Stir eggs, salt, pepper and cayenne pepper together in medium bowl. Pour over cheese.

Arrange tomato slices on top, overlapping if necessary. Bake, uncovered, in 350°F (175°C) oven for about 30 minutes until set. Serves 4.

1 serving: 289 Calories; 20.4 g Total Fat; 1422 mg Sodium; 20 g Protein; 7 g Carbohydrate; 1 g Dietary Fiber

SHRIMP FRITTATA

Make this for brunch, lunch or dinner. Fresh fruit makes an excellent accompaniment.

Day-old bread slices	6	6
Small cooked shrimp	8 oz.	225 g
Grated light sharp Cheddar cheese	½ cup	125 mL
Finely diced green or red pepper	¼ cup	60 mL
Frozen egg product, thawed (see Note)	1 cup	250 mL
Dijon mustard	2 tsp.	10 mL
Celery salt	½ tsp.	2 mL
Can of skim evaporated milk	13½ oz.	385 mL
Skim milk	⅓ cup	75 mL
Crisp rice cereal	½ cup	125 mL
Grated light sharp Cheddar cheese	½ cup	125 mL
Paprika, sprinkle		

Lightly grease 9 inch (22 cm) round glass baking dish or 2 quart (2 L) casserole. Cut bread slices into ½ inch (12 mm) cubes. Place ½ in bottom of dish. Sprinkle with shrimp, first amount of cheese and pepper. Top with remaining bread cubes.

Combine egg product, mustard, celery salt and both milks in medium bowl. Pour over bread cubes, pressing down lightly. Bake, uncovered, in 350°F (175°C) oven for 45 minutes.

Combine cereal and second amount of cheese. Sprinkle over top. Sprinkle with paprika. Bake, uncovered, for 15 minutes until cheese is melted. Let stand for 5 minutes before serving. Serves 6.

1 serving: 265 Calories; 5.9 g Total Fat; 678 mg Sodium; 26 g Protein; 26 g Carbohydrate; 1 g Dietary Fiber

Pictured on page 53.

Note: 4 tbsp. (60 mL) frozen egg product = 1 large egg.

HEARTY FRITTATA

Contains beans and turkey wieners. To make meatless, simply use tofu wieners.

Large eggs	6	6
Can of red kidney beans, drained and rinsed	14 oz.	398 mL
Milk	¾ cup	175 mL
Grated Gouda (or Havarti) cheese	½ cup	125 mL
Chopped turkey wieners (or pepperoni)	1 cup	250 mL
Finely chopped green pepper	3 tbsp.	50 mL
Chopped chives	1 tbsp.	15 mL
Dried sweet basil	½ tsp.	2 mL
Garlic powder	¼ tsp.	1 mL
Salt	¼ tsp.	1 mL
Pepper, sprinkle	¼ tsp.	1 mL

Beat eggs together in medium bowl until smooth.

Stir in remaining 10 ingredients. Pour into greased 3 quart (3 L) casserole or 10 inch (25 cm) quiche pan. Bake, uncovered, in 350°F (175°C) oven for 40 to 45 minutes until set. Serves 6.

1 serving: 227 Calories; 11.7 g Total Fat; 792 mg Sodium; 16 g Protein; 14 g Carbohydrate; 4 g Dietary Fiber

For best results, egg whites should always be room temperature before beating.

MUSHROOM FRITTATA

Spices and Parmesan cheese add heaps of flavor.

Margarine (or butter)	1½ tbsp.	25 mL
Sliced fresh mushrooms	3 cups	750 mL
Large eggs	6	6
Water	3 tbsp.	50 mL
Grated Edam cheese	½ cup	125 mL
Grated Parmesan cheese	2 tbsp.	30 mL
Ground thyme	⅛ tsp.	0.5 mL
Salt	¼ tsp.	1 mL
Pepper, sprinkle		
Paprika, sprinkle		

Melt margarine in 10 inch (25 cm) non-stick frying pan. Add mushrooms. Sauté until moisture is evaporated.

Beat eggs in small bowl.

Add remaining 7 ingredients. Mix. Pour over mushrooms. Stir. Cover. Cook on low for about 20 minutes until set. Cuts into 4 wedges.

1 wedge: 234 Calories; 17.6 g Total Fat; 508 mg Sodium; 15 g Protein; 4 g Carbohydrate; 1 g Dietary Fiber

HAM AND EGG FRITTATA

A panful for two. Add toast to complete your meal.

Cooking oil	1 tsp.	5 mL
Chopped onion	¼ cup	60 mL
Frozen hash brown potatoes	1 cup	250 mL
Diced cooked ham	¼ cup	60 mL
Grated sharp Cheddar cheese	½ cup	125 mL
Large eggs	3	3
Water	1 tbsp.	15 mL
Salt	⅛ tsp.	0.5 mL
Pepper	¹⁄₁₆ tsp.	0.5 mL

Heat cooking oil in 8 inch (20 cm) frying pan. Add onion. Sauté until soft.

Add potatoes. Sauté until tender.

Add ham and cheese. Stir.

Beat eggs, water, salt and pepper in small bowl. Pour over top. Cover. Cook on low for about 15 minutes until set. Serves 2.

1 serving: 354 Calories; 21.3 g Total Fat; 725 mg Sodium; 23 g Protein; 17 g Carbohydrate; 2 g Dietary Fiber

MEDITERRANEAN FRITTATA

Flavor of ham comes through. Zucchini adds texture.

Margarine (or butter)	1 tbsp.	15 mL
Sliced zucchini, with peel	1½ cups	375 mL
Finely chopped onion	¼ cup	60 mL
Can of ham flakes, drained	6½ oz.	184 g
Large eggs	6	6
Water	2 tbsp.	30 mL
Prepared mustard	1 tsp.	5 mL
Lemon juice	1 tsp.	5 mL
Grated mozzarella cheese	½ cup	125 mL
Salt (optional)	¼ tsp.	1 mL

Melt margarine in 10 inch (25 cm) non-stick frying pan. Add zucchini and onion. Sauté until soft.

Add ham. Stir.

Beat eggs in small bowl.

Add remaining 5 ingredients. Mix. Pour over zucchini mixture. Stir. Cover. Cook on low for 20 to 25 minutes until set. Serves 4.

1 serving: 307 Calories; 22.9 g Total Fat; 834 mg Sodium; 21 g Protein; 4 g Carbohydrate; 1 g Dietary Fiber

ARTICHOKE FRITTATA

Contains spinach, cheese and mushrooms—and a hint of sweetness.

Cooking oil	1 tbsp.	15 mL
Chopped onion	2 cups	500 mL
Sliced fresh mushrooms	2 cups	500 mL
Large eggs	9	9
Salt	½ tsp.	2 mL
Pepper	⅛ tsp.	0.5 mL
Ground nutmeg	¹⁄₁₆ tsp.	0.5 mL
Jars of marinated artichoke hearts, (6 oz., 170 mL, each), drained and cut up	2	2
Frozen chopped spinach, thawed and squeezed dry	10 oz.	300 g
Grated medium Cheddar cheese	1 cup	250 mL

Heat cooking oil in 10 inch (25 cm) non-stick frying pan. Add onion and mushrooms. Sauté until soft. This may need to be done in 2 batches.

Beat eggs in medium bowl.

Add remaining 6 ingredients. Add onion and mushrooms. Stir well. Pour into greased 3 quart (3 L) casserole. Bake, uncovered, in 350°F (175°C) oven for about 45 minutes until set. Serves 6.

1 serving: *279 Calories; 17.6 g Total Fat; 617 mg Sodium; 18 g Protein; 14 g Carbohydrate; 5 g Dietary Fiber*

To prevent meat or vegetables from sticking, preheat frying pan first before using. Melt the margarine or butter quickly and then add the meat or vegetables.

POLENTA WEDGES

The secret to a successful polenta is to stir it constantly until very thick.

Can of condensed chicken broth	10 oz.	284 mL
Water	4¾ cups	1.2 L
Cornmeal	1½ cups	375 mL
Grated light Parmesan cheese	¼ cup	60 mL
Dried whole oregano (or Italian spice)	½ tsp.	2 mL
Chopped fresh parsley	¼ cup	60 mL
Finely diced pimiento, drained	2 tbsp.	30 mL
Grated light Parmesan cheese	1 tbsp.	15 mL

Bring broth and water to a boil in non-stick frying pan. Slowly add cornmeal, stirring constantly with whisk. Heat, stirring constantly, for about 25 minutes until mixture is very thick and leaves sides of pan.

Stir in first amount of Parmesan cheese, oregano, parsley and pimiento during last 5 minutes of cooking. Pour mixture into lightly greased 9 inch (22 cm) pie plate. Spread evenly. Cover with plastic wrap. Cool until firm.

Remove to cutting board. Cut evenly into 8 wedges. Arrange wedges individually on foil-lined baking sheet. Lightly grease top of wedges. Sprinkle with second amount of Parmesan cheese. Broil on center rack in oven for about 10 minutes until warm and golden brown. Makes 8 wedges.

1 wedge: *126 Calories; 1.5 g Total Fat; 311 mg Sodium; 6 g Protein; 22 g Carbohydrate; 2 g Dietary Fiber*

Basic Pizza Crust

A crust that will work for any main course.

All-purpose flour	2 cups	500 mL
Instant yeast	1¼ tsp.	6 mL
Salt	¼ tsp.	1 mL
Warm water	⅔ cup	150 mL
Cooking oil	2 tbsp.	30 mL

Food Processor Method: Put first 3 ingredients into food processor fitted with dough blade. With machine running, pour water and cooking oil through feed tube. Process for 50 to 60 seconds. If dough seems sticky to remove, add about ½ tsp. (2 mL) flour.

Hand Method: Put first 3 ingredients into medium bowl. Stir well.

Add warm water and cooking oil. Mix well until dough leaves sides of bowl. Knead on lightly floured surface for 5 to 8 minutes until smooth and elastic.

To Complete: Roll out and press into greased 12 inch (30 cm) pizza pan, forming rim around edges. Or place dough in large greased bowl, turning once to grease top. Cover with tea towel. Let stand in oven with light on and door closed for about 1 hour until doubled in bulk. Punch dough down. Roll out and press into greased 12 inch (30 cm) pizza pan, forming rim around edge.

⅛ crust: 153 Calories; 3.8 g Total Fat; 86 mg Sodium; 4 g Protein; 25 g Carbohydrate; 1 g Dietary Fiber

Pictured on page 36 and on back cover.

THIN BASIC CRUST: Reduce flour to 1½ cups (375 mL) and reduce water to ½ cup (125 mL).

Basic Pizza Sauce

Make your own for a real treat. Freezes well.

Cooking oil	2 tsp.	10 mL
Finely chopped onion	1½ cups	375 mL
Garlic cloves, minced (or ¼-½ tsp., 1-2 mL, garlic powder)	1-2	1-2
Cans of diced tomatoes (19 oz., 540 mL, each), with juice	3	3
Finely chopped celery	⅓ cup	75 mL
Ketchup	2 tbsp.	30 mL
Granulated sugar	½ tsp.	2 mL
Bay leaves	2	2
Ground allspice	¼ tsp.	1 mL
Dried sweet basil	1 tsp.	5 mL
Dried whole oregano	1 tsp.	5 mL
Salt	1 tsp.	5 mL
Pepper	¼ tsp.	1 mL

Heat cooking oil in medium saucepan. Add onion and garlic. Sauté until soft.

Add remaining 10 ingredients. Stir. Heat for about 30 minutes, stirring occasionally, until thickened. Discard bay leaves. Makes 6 cups (1.5 L).

½ cup (125 mL): 61 Calories; 1.3 g Total Fat; 593 mg Sodium; 2 g Protein; 12 g Carbohydrate; 3 g Dietary Fiber

1. Italian Minestrone, page 24
2. Shelled Zucchini Soup, page 27
3. Lentil And Pasta Soup, page 27

ORZO CRUST PIZZA

A unique pizza using orzo pasta as the crust.

Orzo pasta	1 cup	250 mL
Boiling water	4 cups	1 L
Salt	1 tsp.	5 mL
Frozen egg product, thawed	6 tbsp.	100 mL
Grated light Parmesan cheese	2 tbsp.	30 mL
Parsley flakes	2 tsp.	10 mL
Meatless spaghetti sauce	1½ cups	375 mL
Lean ground chicken (or ground beef)	½ lb.	225 g
Seasoned salt	½ tsp.	2 mL
Pepper	¼ tsp.	1 mL
Dried whole oregano	½ tsp.	2 mL
Medium green or red pepper, cut into rings	1	1
Medium red onion, thinly sliced	½	½
Chopped fresh mushrooms	⅔ cup	150 mL
Grated part-skim mozzarella cheese	1 cup	250 mL

Cook pasta in boiling water and salt in large saucepan for 12 to 15 minutes, stirring occasionally, until tender but firm. Drain. Return to saucepan.

Combine egg product, Parmesan cheese and parsley in small bowl. Mix. Pour over pasta. Toss well. Press into greased 12 inch (30 cm) deep dish pizza pan, forming a crust. Spread spaghetti sauce on top almost to edges.

Scramble-fry ground chicken in medium non-stick frying pan until no longer pink. Drain. Add seasoned salt, pepper and oregano. Stir.

Scatter chicken mixture over spaghetti sauce. Cover with green pepper, onion and mushrooms. Sprinkle mozzarella cheese over top. Bake in 400°F (205°C) oven for 20 minutes until cheese is melted and edges are golden. Cuts into 8 wedges.

1 wedge: 223 Calories; 4.6 g Total Fat; 314 mg Sodium; 16 g Protein; 29 g Carbohydrate; 2 g Dietary Fiber

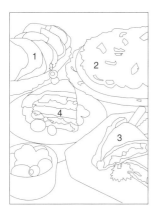

TRADITIONAL PIZZA

If using an unbaked pizza crust, add 10 minutes to the baking time.

Lean ground beef	½ lb.	225 g
Chopped onion	1 cup	250 mL
Sliced fresh mushrooms	2 cups	500 mL
Can of tomato paste (5½ oz., 156 mL)	½	½
Focaccia bread (12 inch, 30 cm, size)	1	1
Dried sweet basil	1 tsp.	5 mL
Dried whole oregano	½ tsp.	2 mL
Grated part-skim mozzarella cheese	1½ cups	375 mL
Grated Asiago cheese	1 cup	250 mL
Medium yellow pepper, cut into rings	1	1
Large tomato, seeded and diced	1	1

Scramble-fry ground beef and onion in non-stick frying pan until beef is browned and onion is soft. Drain. Add mushrooms. Sauté until moisture is evaporated. Spread thin layer of tomato paste on flatbread. Sprinkle with basil and oregano. Layer beef mixture on sauce. Top with both cheeses.

Arrange pepper on top. Sprinkle with tomato. Bake in 425°F (220°C) oven for 10 minutes until hot and cheese is melted. Place under broiler for 3 to 4 minutes to brown cheese if desired. Cuts into 8 wedges.

1 wedge: 319 Calories; 11.3 g Total Fat; 657 mg Sodium; 21 g Protein; 35 g Carbohydrate; 3 g Dietary Fiber

MARGHERITA PIZZA

In honor of Queen Margherita of Italy.

Basic Pizza Crust dough, page 34	1	1
Roma (plum) tomatoes, peeled, seeded and chopped (or can of Italian tomatoes, 14 oz., 398 mL, size, drained and chopped)	1 lb.	454 g
Granulated sugar (optional)	½ tsp.	2 mL
Ground thyme	⅛ tsp.	0.5 mL
Salt	½ tsp.	2 mL
Pepper	⅛ tsp.	0.5 mL
Grated mozzarella cheese	¾ cup	175 mL
Grated Edam cheese	¾ cup	175 mL
Grated Parmesan cheese	2 tbsp.	30 mL
Grated Parmesan cheese	1 tbsp.	15 mL
Chopped fresh sweet basil	½ cup	125 mL

Prepare pizza dough. Roll out and press in greased 12 inch (30 cm) pizza pan, forming rim around edge.

Scatter tomato over crust.

Mix sugar, thyme, salt and pepper in small cup. Sprinkle over tomato.

Sprinkle mozzarella cheese, Edam cheese and first amount of Parmesan cheese over top. Bake on bottom rack in 425°F (220°C) oven for about 15 minutes, or for about 8 minutes if using partially baked crust.

Sprinkle with second amount of Parmesan cheese and basil. Cuts into 8 wedges.

1 wedge: 245 Calories; 9.6 g Total Fat; 465 mg Sodium; 11 g Protein; 29 g Carbohydrate; 2 g Dietary Fiber

FOCACCIA

This loaf knows no bounds. Use one of the listed toppings or make up your own. Foh-KAH-chee-ah is a fun loaf.

Granulated sugar	1 tsp.	5 mL
Warm water	¼ cup	60 mL
Envelope of active dry yeast (1 tbsp., 15 mL)	¼ oz.	8 g
All-purpose flour	3¼ cups	800 mL
Salt	1 tsp.	5 mL
Olive oil	2 tsp.	10 mL
Water	1 cup	250 mL

TOPPING 1

Small red onion, halved lengthwise and thinly sliced	1	1
Olive oil	2 tbsp.	30 mL
Coarse (or sea) salt, sprinkle		

TOPPING 2

Olive oil	2 tbsp.	30 mL
Ground rosemary	1 tsp.	5 mL
Dried thyme	¼ tsp.	1 mL
Ground sage	¼ tsp.	1 mL
Dried whole oregano	¼ tsp.	1 mL
Coarse (or sea) salt, sprinkle		

TOPPING 3

Olive oil	2 tbsp.	30 mL
Dried sweet basil	¼ tsp.	1 mL
Garlic powder	¼ tsp.	1 mL
Ground pecans	1 tbsp.	15 mL
Coarse (or sea) salt, sprinkle		

Stir sugar and warm water together in small bowl. Sprinkle yeast over top. Let stand for 10 minutes. Stir to dissolve yeast.

Measure flour and salt into large bowl. Stir. Make a well in center. Add yeast mixture to well. Stir with spoon until mixed. Make a well once more.

Add olive oil and remaining water to well. Stir. Turn out onto floured surface. Knead for 8 to 10 minutes until smooth and elastic. Place in greased bowl, turning once to grease top. Cover with tea towel. Let stand in oven with light on and door closed for 1 to 1½ hours until doubled in bulk. Punch down dough. Place on greased baking sheet. Press or roll out to 12 inch (30 cm) circle. Makes 1 round flat loaf.

Topping 1: Soak red onion in cold water for 30 minutes. Drain. Pat dry. Arrange on top of loaf. Press onion down with fingers, making dents. Drizzle with olive oil, allowing it to pool in dents.

Sprinkle with salt. Let stand, uncovered, for 30 minutes. Bake in 400°F (205°C) oven for about 25 minutes. Serve warm or cold. Cuts into 8 wedges.

1 wedge: 244 Calories; 5.1 g Total Fat; 341 mg Sodium; 6 g Protein; 43 g Carbohydrate; 2 g Dietary Fiber

Topping 2: Make dents with finger in surface of loaf. Drizzle with olive oil, allowing it to pool in dents. Mix rosemary, thyme, sage and oregano in small bowl. Sprinkle over top. Finish as in Topping 1. Cuts into 8 wedges.

1 wedge: 241 Calories; 5.1 g Total Fat; 341 mg Sodium; 6 g Protein; 42 g Carbohydrate; 2 g Dietary Fiber

Topping 3: Make dents with fingers in surface of loaf. Drizzle with olive oil, allowing it to pool in dents. Mix basil, garlic powder and pecans in small bowl. Sprinkle over top. Finish as in Topping 1. Cuts into 8 wedges.

1 wedge: 246 Calories; 5.6 g Total Fat; 341 mg Sodium; 6 g Protein; 42 g Carbohydrate; 2 g Dietary Fiber

PESTO, CHICKEN AND PEPPER FOCACCIA

Wonderful pesto and pepper flavor on this thick-crusted pizza.

Boneless, skinless chicken breast halves (about 2)	½ lb.	225 g
Salt, sprinkle		
Freshly ground pepper, sprinkle		
Medium red pepper, halved	½	½
Olive oil	2 tsp.	10 mL
Focaccia bread (12 inch, 30 cm, size)	1	1
Basil Pesto, page 91	2 tbsp.	30 mL
Grated Asiago (or part-part skim mozzarella) cheese	⅓ cup	75 mL
Grated Parmesan cheese	1 tbsp.	15 mL

Preheat barbecue to high. Sprinkle chicken with salt and pepper. Place chicken and red pepper, skin side down, on greased grill. Close lid. Cook for 8 to 10 minutes, turning chicken after 5 minutes but leaving pepper, skin side down, to blacken. Remove chicken. Cut into thin diagonal slices. Remove red pepper to bowl. Cover with plastic wrap until cool enough to handle. Peel off blackened skin and discard. Cut pepper into slivers.

Brush part of olive oil on bottom of focaccia. Combine remaining olive oil and pesto in small cup. Spread on top of focaccia to edges. Arrange chicken and red pepper on pesto. Sprinkle both cheeses over top. Turn barbecue to medium. Place focaccia on greased grill. Cook for about 2 minutes until bottom is browned. Turn off heat but leave opposite burner on. Close lid. Let stand for 5 minutes until cheese is melted. Cuts into 8 wedges.

1 wedge: 230 Calories; 4.6 g Total Fat; 386 mg Sodium; 13 g Protein; 33 g Carbohydrate; 1 g Dietary Fiber

SEAFOOD FOCACCIA

A super simple snack or, foh-KAH-chee-ah can be served for lunch.

Cooking oil	2 tbsp.	30 mL
Finely chopped onion	¾ cup	175 mL
Small green pepper, diced	1	1
Diced fresh mushrooms	¾ cup	175 mL
Garlic clove, minced	1	1
Large shrimp, peeled and deveined	12	12
Large scallops, sliced in half	12	12
Focaccia bread (12 inch, 30 cm, size)	1	1
Basil Pesto, page 91	1 cup	250 mL
Diced pitted ripe olives	¾ cup	175 mL
Crumbled feta cheese	1 cup	250 mL

Heat cooking oil in frying pan. Add onion, green pepper, mushrooms and garlic. Sauté for about 3 minutes.

Add shrimp and scallops. Stir-fry until shrimp turns pinkish and curls a bit and scallops are white and opaque. Remove from heat.

Put focaccia loaf on ungreased baking sheet. Spread with pesto. Layer shrimp-scallop mixture on top. Add olives, then cheese. Bake in 350°F (175°C) oven for 15 to 20 minutes. Serves 2.

1 serving: 764 Calories; 30.7 g Total Fat; 1107 mg Sodium; 27 g Protein; 94 g Carbohydrate; 6 g Dietary Fiber

★★★★★★★★★★★★★★★★★★★★★★★★★★★★

ROASTED VEGETABLE FOCACCIA

So eye-catching! So delicious! So easy! This foh-KAH-chee-ah takes only 30 minutes from start to finish.

Medium red onion, thinly sliced	½	½
Sliced fresh mushrooms	2 cups	500 mL
Yellow or orange pepper, slivered	1	1
Roma (plum) tomatoes, chopped	2	2
Olive oil	½ tsp.	2 mL
Balsamic vinegar	2 tbsp.	30 mL
Small garlic clove, crushed	1	1
Chopped fresh sweet basil	2 tbsp.	30 mL
Freshly ground pepper	¼ tsp.	1 mL
Focaccia bread (12 inch, 30 cm, size)	1	1
Grated part-skim mozzarella cheese	1 cup	250 mL

Combine first 4 ingredients in large bowl.

Whisk olive oil, vinegar, garlic, basil and pepper in small bowl. Pour over vegetables. Toss. Place in single layer on large ungreased baking sheet with sides. Bake, uncovered, in 500°F (260°C) oven on top rack for 10 minutes until vegetables are tender.

Reduce heat to 450°F (230°C). Arrange vegetables evenly on focaccia, spreading to edges. Sprinkle with cheese. Place on large pizza pan or directly on center rack in oven. Bake for 8 to 10 minutes until cheese is melted and crust is crispy. Cuts into 8 wedges.

1 wedge: 168 Calories; 3.8 g Total Fat; 546 mg Sodium; 8 g Protein; 26 g Carbohydrate; 2 g Dietary Fiber

Pictured on page 36 and on back cover.

ITALIAN FOCACCIA SANDWICHES

A sandwich never tasted so good.

Focaccia bread (10 inch, 25 cm, size)	1	1
Sun-dried tomato pesto	2 tbsp.	30 mL
Thin slices provolone cheese (about 6 oz., 170 g)	12	12
Paper-thin slices red onion	6	6
Paper-thin slices prosciutto (or ham), about 12 oz., 340 g	12	12
Diced green pepper	6 tbsp.	100 mL
Non-fat Italian dressing	6 tbsp.	100 mL

Preheat lightly sprayed 2-sided electric grill for 5 minutes. Split focaccia in half horizontally. Spread each cut side with thin coating of pesto.

Place 6 slices of cheese on pesto on bottom half of focaccia. Layer red onion and prosciutto on cheese. Sprinkle green pepper over all.

Drizzle with dressing. Top with remaining 6 slices of cheese. Cover with top half of focaccia. Cut into 8 wedges. Place 2 wedges on grill. Close lid. Cook for 5 minutes until bread is toasted and cheese is melted inside. Repeat with remaining wedges. Makes 8 sandwiches.

1 sandwich: 567 Calories; 41.5 g Total Fat; 1252 mg Sodium; 13 g Protein; 34 g Carbohydrate; 1 g Dietary Fiber

ITALIAN CHEESE BREAD

This bread is incredible. One slice is never enough.

All-purpose flour	2½ cups	625 mL
Granulated sugar	¼ cup	60 mL
Envelopes of active dry yeast (¼ oz., 8 g, each)	2	2
Salt	1½ tsp.	7 mL
Milk	1 cup	250 mL
Water	1 cup	250 mL
Margarine (or butter)	½ cup	125 mL
Large eggs	2	2
All-purpose flour, approximately	2¾ cups	675 mL
FILLING		
Grated mozzarella cheese	1 cup	250 mL
Margarine (or butter), softened	¼ cup	60 mL
Envelope of Italian dressing and dip mix	1½ oz.	42 g
Garlic powder	¼ tsp.	1 mL
Sesame seeds	2 tbsp.	30 mL

Place first 4 ingredients in large bowl. Stir well.

Heat milk, water and margarine in saucepan until quite warm and margarine is melted. Add to yeast mixture.

Add eggs. Beat on low to moisten. Beat on medium for 3 minutes.

Work in enough remaining flour to make stiff batter.

Filling: Mix first 4 ingredients well in small bowl.

Grease 12 cup (2.7 L) bundt pan well. Sprinkle with sesame seeds. Spoon ½ of batter into pan. Spoon filling over top, to within about ½ inch (12 mm) from sides. Spoon remaining batter over filling. Cover with greased waxed paper and tea towel. Let rise in oven with light on and door closed for about 30 minutes until doubled in bulk. Bake in 350°F (175°C) oven for about 30 minutes until golden brown. Bread will sound hollow when tapped with knuckle. Immediately remove from pan to rack to cool. Serve warm or cold. Makes 1 loaf. Cuts into 24 slices.

1 slice: *208 Calories; 8.8 g Total Fat; 331 mg Sodium; 6 g Protein; 26 g Carbohydrate; 1 g Dietary Fiber*

To use pasta in a salad, rinse cooked pasta with cold water. Rinsing with cold water stops the cooking of the pasta and ensures that it will remain firm.

Layered Italian Loaf

A make-ahead sandwich. Great for picnics!
Include olives and pickled onions on each plate.

Olive oil	⅓ cup	75 mL
Red wine vinegar	2 tbsp.	30 mL
Roma (plum) tomatoes, seeded and diced	4	4
Dried sweet basil	1 tbsp.	15 mL
Garlic cloves, minced	3	3
Jar of pimiento, with liquid, chopped	2 oz.	57 mL
Finely chopped green pepper	½ cup	125 mL
Finely chopped red pepper	½ cup	125 mL
Chopped pitted ripe olives	½ cup	125 mL
Round Italian bread loaf (10 inch, 25 cm, size)	1	1
Grated Swiss cheese	½ cup	125 mL
Grated provolone cheese	½ cup	125 mL
Deli (or cooked lean) beef, very thinly sliced	½ lb.	225 g

Combine first 9 ingredients in medium bowl.
Cover. Marinate at room temperature for 1 to
2 hours.

Cut loaf in half horizontally. Remove 1 inch
(2.5 cm) layer from inside of each half, leaving
1 inch (2.5 cm) border around top edge. Pour
3 tbsp. (50 mL) juice from tomato mixture into
small bowl. Brush juice over cut surface on both
halves of loaf. Spread tomato mixture and
remaining juice evenly over both halves.

Divide both cheeses on tomato mixture. Lay beef
on bottom half only. Pack both fillings down
slightly. Carefully turn top half onto bottom half.
Press down firmly on loaf. Wrap tightly in plastic
wrap. Chill loaf overnight with something heavy
on top to keep loaf slightly flattened. Cuts into
8 wedges.

1 wedge: 367 Calories; 15.7 g Total Fat; 520 mg Sodium;
18 g Protein; 38 g Carbohydrate; 2 g Dietary Fiber

Pictured on page 36 and on back cover.

Italian Bread

Contains straht-CHEE-noh cheese. Cream cheese
may be substituted. Also contains pro-SHOO-toh.

Granulated sugar	1 tsp.	5 mL
Warm milk	¼ cup	60 mL
Envelope of active dry yeast	¼ oz.	8 g
Stracchino (or cream) cheese, softened	4 oz.	125 g
Large eggs	3	3
Olive oil	3 tbsp.	50 mL
Grated Romano cheese	½ cup	125 mL
Chopped prosciutto (or cooked ham)	1½ cups	375 mL
Pepper	¼ tsp.	1 mL
All-purpose flour, approximately	2⅔ cups	650 mL
Milk, for brushing top	2 tsp.	10 mL

Stir sugar in warm milk in small bowl. Sprinkle
yeast over top. Let stand for 10 minutes. Stir to
dissolve yeast.

Beat Stracchino cheese and eggs in large bowl.
Mix in olive oil and Romano cheese. Add
prosciutto and pepper. Stir. Add yeast mixture. Stir.

Work in enough flour until dough pulls away from
sides of bowl. Turn out onto floured surface.
Knead 8 to 10 minutes until smooth and elastic.
Place in greased bowl, turning once to grease top.
Cover with tea towel. Let stand in oven with light
on and door closed for 1 to 1½ hours until doubled
in bulk. Punch dough down. Place in greased
1½ quart (1.5 L) casserole. Cover with tea towel.
Let stand in oven with light on and door closed for
about 45 minutes until doubled in size.

Brush top with milk. Bake in 375°F (190°C) oven
for about 35 minutes. Turn out onto rack to cool.
Makes 1 loaf. Cuts into 12 slices.

1 slice: 247 Calories; 11.4 g Total Fat; 378 mg Sodium;
11 g Protein; 24 g Carbohydrate; 1 g Dietary Fiber

Pictured on page 36 and on back cover.

HAM AND CHEESE CALZONES

Very colorful filling in this hearty cross between a sandwich and a pizza. Serve with carrot and celery sticks.

Basic Pizza Crust dough, page 34	1	1
Cooking oil	2 tsp.	10 mL
Chopped green pepper	½ cup	125 mL
Chopped red pepper	½ cup	125 mL
Can of sliced mushrooms, drained	10 oz.	284 mL
Garlic powder	¼ tsp.	1 mL
Salt	¼ tsp.	1 mL
Pepper	¹⁄₁₆ tsp.	0.5 mL
Basic Pizza Sauce, page 34	¼ cup	60 mL
Can of ham flakes, drained and crumbled	6½ oz.	184 g
Grated Parmesan cheese	4 tsp.	20 mL
Grated Muenster cheese	1 cup	250 mL

Prepare pizza dough. Divide into 4 equal balls. Cover. Let rest while preparing filling.

Sauté green and red peppers in hot cooking oil in medium frying pan until tender-crisp. Remove from heat.

Add mushrooms, garlic powder, salt and pepper. Stir together.

Roll out 1 ball of dough on lightly floured surface into ⅛ inch (3 mm) thick circle. Spread ½ of circle with 1 tbsp. (15 mL) pizza sauce, to within 1 inch (2.5 cm) of edge. Spoon ¼ of mushroom mixture over top of pizza sauce. Layer with ¼ of ham. Sprinkle with 1 tsp. (5 mL) Parmesan cheese and ¼ cup (60 mL) Muenster cheese. Moisten edge with water. Fold over and press to seal, folding edge upward and over. Crimp edge with fork. Repeat, making 3 more. Place on greased baking sheet. Poke holes in top. Bake on bottom rack in 425°F (220°C) oven for about 15 minutes. Makes 4 calzones.

1 calzone: 569 Calories; 28.8 g Total Fat; 1425 mg Sodium; 25 g Protein; 55 g Carbohydrate; 7 g Dietary Fiber

Pictured on page 36 and on back cover.

BEEF CALZONES

This could easily be one of your favorites.

Basic Pizza Crust dough, page 34	1	1
Beef stew meat, cubed	¾ lb.	340 g
Cooking oil	2 tsp.	10 mL
Water, to cover		
Salt	½ tsp.	2 mL
Pepper	⅛ tsp.	0.5 mL
Chopped onion	½ cup	125 mL
Basic Pizza Sauce, page 34	¼ cup	60 mL
Can of asparagus tips, drained	12 oz.	341 mL
Grated part-skim mozzarella cheese	1⅓ cups	325 mL

Prepare pizza dough. Divide into 4 equal balls. Cover. Let rest while preparing filling.

Brown stew meat in hot cooking oil in medium frying pan. Spoon into large saucepan.

Pour 1 cup (250 mL) water into frying pan. Loosen all browned bits. Pour over beef. Add water to cover, salt and pepper. Bring to a boil. Reduce heat. Cover. Simmer for 1 hour.

Add onion. Simmer for 30 minutes. Strain, saving broth for soup if you like. Spread stew meat mixture on large plate to cool.

Roll out 1 ball of dough on lightly floured surface into ⅛ inch (3 mm) thick circle. Spread ½ of circle with ¼ of sauce, to within 1 inch (2.5 cm) of edge. Spoon ¼ of beef mixture over sauce. Lay about 5 asparagus tips, side by side, on top. Sprinkle with ⅓ cup (75 mL) cheese. Moisten edge with water. Fold over and press to seal, folding edge upward and over. Crimp edge with fork. Repeat, making 3 more. Place on greased baking sheet. Poke holes in top. Bake on bottom rack in 425°F (220°C) oven for about 15 minutes. Makes 4 calzones.

1 calzone: 596 Calories; 23.2 g Total Fat; 1165 mg Sodium; 38 g Protein; 58 g Carbohydrate; 4 g Dietary Fiber

Main Dishes

There's so many choices for entrées in Italian, you'll wonder which to try first. Why not make Lazy Ravioli, page 52, at the end of a work day? Stuff your own Tortellini, page 48, with meat or mushrooms, and serve with Pasta and Lemon Vegetables, page 75, for a double delight for family or friends. Roasted Chicken and Vegetables, page 64, or Veal Marsala, page 60, have all the makings for a contented crew at your house.

SEAFOOD ITALIA

A golden top with pimiento, shrimp and mushrooms visible. Good choice.

Elbow macaroni (about 8 oz., 225 g)	2 cups	500 mL
Cooking oil	1 tbsp.	15 mL
Salt	2 tsp.	10 mL
Water	12 cups	3 L
Cans of condensed cream of mushroom soup (10 oz., 284 mL, each)	2	2
Milk	1 cup	250 mL
Crabmeat (or 1 can of crabmeat, 4¼ oz., 120 g, drained), membrane removed	1 cup	250 mL
Small cooked shrimp (or 1 can of shrimp, 4 oz., 113 g, drained and rinsed)	1 cup	250 mL
Can of mushroom pieces, drained	10 oz.	284 mL
Diced pimiento	¼ cup	60 mL
Grated Parmesan cheese	½ cup	125 mL
Garlic salt	1 tsp.	5 mL
Cayenne pepper	⅛ tsp.	0.5 mL
Grated Parmesan cheese	½ cup	125 mL
Margarine (or butter)	2 tbsp.	30 mL

Cook macaroni, in cooking oil and salt in boiling water in large uncovered pot or Dutch oven for 5 to 7 minutes, stirring occasionally, until tender but firm. Drain. Return to pot.

Heat and stir soup and milk in medium saucepan.

Add next 7 ingredients. Stir. Add to macaroni. Stir. Turn into ungreased 3 quart (3 L) casserole.

Sprinkle with second amount of cheese. Dot with bits of margarine. Bake, uncovered, in 350°F (175°C) oven for about 30 minutes until hot and bubbly. Serves 6.

1 serving: 415 Calories; 18.3 g Total Fat; 1595 mg Sodium; 22 g Protein; 40 g Carbohydrate; 2 g Dietary Fiber

Pictured on front cover.

LINGUINE WITH SMOKED SALMON AND OLIVE

Easy and quick to prepare. Garlic and wine flavors complement the salmon.

Garlic clove, minced	1	1
Finely chopped onion	¼ cup	60 mL
Olive oil	1 tsp.	5 mL
Smoked salmon, diced or cut into strips	5 oz.	140 g
Water	¼ cup	60 mL
Dry white (or alcohol-free) wine	¼ cup	60 mL
Chopped fresh parsley (or 1 tsp., 5 mL, flakes)	1 tbsp.	15 mL
Chopped fresh dill (or ½ tsp., 2 mL, dried)	1½ tsp.	7 mL
Seafood (or vegetable) bouillon powder	½ tsp.	2 mL
Freshly ground pepper, sprinkle		
Dried crushed chilies, sprinkle		
Chopped pitted ripe olives	1 tbsp.	15 mL
Linguine pasta	8 oz.	225 g
Boiling water	8 cups	2 L
Salt	2 tsp.	10 mL

Sauté garlic and onion in olive oil in medium frying pan for about 2 minutes until onion is soft.

Stir in next 9 ingredients. Cover. Keep warm on low.

Cook pasta in boiling water and salt in large uncovered pot or Dutch oven for 8 to 10 minutes, stirring occasionally, until tender but firm. Drain. Return to pot. Add sauce. Toss to coat. Serve immediately. Serves 4.

1 serving: 280 Calories; 3.8 g Total Fat; 799 mg Sodium; 14 g Protein; 44 g Carbohydrate; 2 g Dietary Fiber

SHRIMP TETRAZZINI

Great luncheon casserole.

Margarine (or butter)	¼ cup	60 mL
Chopped green onion	¼ cup	125 mL
Sliced fresh mushrooms	1 cup	250 mL
All-purpose flour	3 tbsp.	50 mL
Chicken bouillon powder	1 tbsp.	15 mL
Garlic powder	¼ tsp.	1 mL
Milk	1½ cups	375 mL
Dry white (or alcohol-free) wine	¼ cup	60 mL
Medium egg noodles	8 oz.	225 g
Cooking oil (optional)	1 tbsp.	15 mL
Salt	2 tsp.	10 mL
Boiling water	10 cups	2.5 L
Medium cooked shrimp	2 cups	500 mL
Grated Swiss cheese	1 cup	250 mL
Grated Parmesan cheese	¼ cup	60 mL

Melt margarine in frying pan or large saucepan. Add green onion and mushrooms. Sauté until soft.

Mix in flour, bouillon powder and garlic powder. Add milk. Heat and stir until boiling and thickened. Stir in wine. Remove from heat.

Cook noodles in cooking oil and salt in boiling water in large uncovered pot or Dutch oven for 5 to 7 minutes, stirring occasionally, until tender but firm. Drain. Combine with sauce.

Add shrimp. Toss together. Turn into greased 2 quart (2 L) casserole.

Sprinkle both cheeses over top. Bake, uncovered, in 350°F (175°C) oven for 25 to 30 minutes until hot and golden. Serves 4.

1 serving: 637 Calories; 26.5 g Total Fat; 1041 mg Sodium; 39 g Protein; 58 g Carbohydrate; 2 g Dietary Fiber

FAST SEAFOOD PASTA

Lots of color with showy bow pasta. This is an exceptional recipe for company.

Medium bow pasta (about 8 oz., 225 g)	2⅔ cups	650 mL
Salt	1 tbsp.	15 mL
Boiling water	12 cups	3 L
Chopped onion	¼ cup	60 mL
Diced celery	¼ cup	60 mL
Chopped fresh mushrooms	½ cup	125 mL
Garlic clove, minced	1	1
Diced red pepper	½ cup	125 mL
Diced zucchini, with peel	½ cup	125 mL
Chili sauce	¼ cup	60 mL
Frozen medium raw shrimp (about 8 oz., 225 g)	1½ cups	375 mL
Frozen bay (small) scallops (about 8 oz.,225 g)	1 cup	250 mL
Cooking oil	2 tsp.	10 mL
Chopped fresh sweet basil (or 2 tsp., 10 mL, dried)	2 tbsp.	30 mL
Chopped fresh parsley (or 1 tsp., 5 mL, flakes)	1 tbsp.	15 mL
Salt	¼ tsp.	1 mL
Pepper, sprinkle		
Cayenne pepper, sprinkle		

Cook pasta and first amount of salt in boiling water in large uncovered pot or Dutch oven for 7 to 9 minutes, stirring occasionally, until tender but firm. Drain well. Return to pot.

Toss next 7 ingredients in small bowl. Set aside.

Preheat lightly sprayed 2-sided electric grill for 5 minutes. Toss shrimp, scallops, cooking oil, basil, parsley, second amount of salt, pepper and cayenne pepper in large bowl. Turn out vegetable mixture onto grill. Close lid. Cook for 3 minutes. Add seafood mixture. Close lid. Cook for 7 minutes. Toss seafood mixture with pasta, plus juices from frying pan. Serves 4.

1 serving: 374 Calories; 4.8 g Total Fat; 600 mg Sodium; 29 g Protein; 52 g Carbohydrate; 4 g Dietary Fiber

CREAMY MUSSELS 'N' PASTA

This pasta uses a thin sauce that tastes very rich and creamy.

Penne pasta (about 10 oz., 285 g)	3½ cups	875 mL
Boiling water	16 cups	4 L
Salt	4 tsp.	20 mL
Garlic cloves, minced	3	3
Finely chopped onion	½ cup	125 mL
Dried crushed chilies	⅛ tsp.	0.5 mL
Cayenne pepper	¹⁄₁₆ tsp.	0.5 mL
Olive oil	2 tsp.	10 mL
Can of red peppers, drained and finely diced	14 oz.	398 mL
Dry white (or alcohol-free) wine	½ cup	125 mL
Light spreadable cream cheese	2 tbsp.	30 mL
Fresh mussels (about 30), beards removed and scrubbed clean (see Note)	2¼ lbs.	1 kg
Green onions, sliced	2	2
Chopped fresh parsley	2 tbsp.	30 mL

Cook pasta in boiling water and salt in large uncovered pot or Dutch oven for 10 to 12 minutes, stirring occasionally, until tender but firm. Drain. Rinse with warm water. Drain.

Sauté garlic, onion, chilies and cayenne pepper in olive oil in large non-stick wok for 2 minutes until onion is soft. Add red pepper. Sauté for 2 minutes.

Stir in wine and cream cheese. Bring to a boil. Add mussels. Reduce heat. Cover. Simmer for 3 minutes until shells are opened. Add pasta, green onion and parsley. Stir gently. Cover. Cook for 1 minute until pasta is warm. Discard any mussels that remain closed. Serve immediately. Serves 4.

1 serving: 395 Calories; 6 g Total Fat; 313 mg Sodium; 17 g Protein; 62 g Carbohydrate; 3 g Dietary Fiber

Note: Before cooking, discard any mussels that are open or remain open when sharply tapped.

TORTELLINI

These little gems are served in a creamy sauce.
For a spicier dish, serve with a tomato sauce.

TORTELLINI

All-purpose flour	**2 cups**	**500 mL**
Large eggs	**4**	**4**
Salt	**½ tsp.**	**2 mL**
Boiling water	**16 cups**	**4 L**

MEAT FILLING

Finely chopped cooked	**1 cup**	**250 mL**
pork (or chicken)		
Grated Parmesan cheese	**3 tbsp.**	**50 mL**
Large egg	**1**	**1**
Salt	**¼ tsp.**	**1 mL**
Pepper, sprinkle		

PARMESAN SAUCE

Whipping cream	**1 cup**	**250 mL**
Margarine (or butter)	**1 tbsp.**	**15 mL**
Grated Parmesan cheese	**⅔ cup**	**150 mL**
Chopped fresh parsley	**¼ cup**	**60 mL**
Salt	**⅛ tsp.**	**0.5 mL**

Freshly ground pepper, for garnish

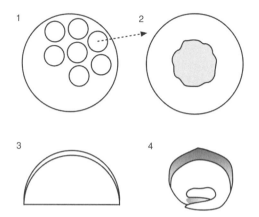

Tortellini: Mix flour, eggs and salt to form stiff dough. Divide into 4 balls.

1. Roll out ¼ of rested dough into very thin large circle. Cut about 12-2 inch (5 cm) circles of dough.
2. On each circle, place rounded ¼ tsp. (1 mL) filling in center. Moisten half of circle with water.
3. Fold dough over filling to seal edges.
4. Bend fold over finger and join 2 ends together. Repeat with remaining dough and filling. Place pasta on floured tray. Cover with damp tea towel until ready to cook. Makes about 48 tortellini.

Cook tortellini in 3 batches in boiling water in large uncovered pot or Dutch oven for 4 to 5 minutes, stirring occasionally, until tender but firm. Remove with sieve or slotted spoon to colander. Rinse with hot water. Drain. Place in serving dish.

Meat filling: Mix all 5 ingredients in small bowl. Add a bit of water if needed, to hold together. Makes 1 cup (250 mL) filling.

Parmesan Sauce: Combine all 5 ingredients in small saucepan. Mix. Bring to a simmer on low. Pour over tortellini. Makes 1½ cups (375 mL) sauce.

Garnish with pepper. Serves 8.

1 serving with ⅓ cup (75 mL) sauce: 739 Calories;
41.2 g Total Fat; 1178 mg Sodium; 36 g Protein;
54 g Carbohydrate; 2 g Dietary Fiber

Pictured on page 54.

MUSHROOM FILLING

Garlic clove, minced	**1**	**1**
Finely chopped onion	**½ cup**	**125 mL**
Margarine (or butter)	**2 tsp.**	**10 mL**
Chopped fresh mushrooms	**2 cups**	**500 mL**

(continued on next page)

Non-fat spreadable cream cheese	2 tbsp.	30 mL
Seasoned salt	1 tsp.	5 mL
Pepper, sprinkle		
Parsley flakes	2 tsp.	10 mL
Dried thyme, crushed	¼ tsp.	1 mL
Egg whites (large)	2	2
Fine dry bread crumbs	⅓ cup	75 mL

Mushroom Filling: Sauté garlic and onion in margarine for 1 minute. Add mushrooms. Sauté until soft. Cool mixture slightly.

Put mushroom mixture into blender. Add cream cheese, seasoned salt, pepper, parsley, thyme and egg whites. Process until smooth. Remove to medium bowl. Add bread crumbs. Mix well. Makes about 1 cup (250 mL) filling.

HERB BUTTER

Olive oil	1 tsp.	5 mL
Butter (or margarine)	3 tbsp.	50 mL
Garlic clove, minced	1	1
Finely chopped fresh parsley, packed	¼ cup	60 mL
Finely chopped fresh sweet basil, packed	¼ cup	60 mL
Finely chopped fresh dill, packed	2 tbsp.	30 mL
Finely chopped fresh oregano, packed	2 tbsp.	30 mL
Salt	¼ tsp.	1 mL

Grated Parmesan Cheese, sprinkle

Herb Butter: Combine first 8 ingredients in small bowl. Let stand for 10 minutes to allow flavors to blend. Pour over tortellini. Toss lightly.

Sprinkle with Parmesan cheese. Makes about ⅔ cup (150 mL) butter.

1 serving mushroom tortellini with 2 tbsp. (30 mL) herb butter: 266 Calories; 4.6 g Total Fat; 765 mg Sodium; 11 g Protein; 45 g Carbohydrate; 2 g Dietary Fiber

CREAMY TORTELLINI

Get the good meal without all the work to make the tortellini. Excellent.

Frozen tortellini	1 lb.	454 g
Boiling water	16 cups	4 L
Half-and-half cream	2 cups	500 mL
Grated carrot	½ cup	125 mL
Minced onion flakes	2 tbsp.	30 mL
Celery leaves	1 tbsp.	15 mL
Parsley flakes	1 tsp.	5 mL
Garlic powder	¼ tsp.	1 mL
Chicken bouillon powder	2 tsp.	10 mL
Salt	½ tsp.	2 mL
Pepper	⅛ tsp.	0.5 mL
Grated Parmesan cheese	¼ cup	60 mL

Cook tortellini in boiling water in large uncovered pot or Dutch oven for 8 to 14 minutes, stirring occasionally, until tender but firm.

Measure next 9 ingredients into medium saucepan. Bring to a boil on medium. Reduce heat. Simmer for about 5 minutes until carrot is tender.

Add tortellini. Stir in Parmesan cheese. Serves 4.

1 serving: 615 Calories; 25.9 g Total Fat; 1427 mg Sodium; 32 g Protein; 62 g Carbohydrate; 3 g Dietary Fiber

For pasta that isn't starchy and sticky, cook in at least 8 cups (2 L) for every 8 oz. (225 g) of pasta. This allows the pasta to expand and not stick together.

CHORIZO AND ROTINI DINNER

This dinner is served warm with a pleasant heat coming from the sausage.

Spicy chorizo sausages	½ lb.	225 g
Medium green pepper, quartered	1	1
Medium onion, peeled, root end intact, cut into 6 wedges	1	1
Garlic cloves, minced	2	2
Olive oil	1½ tsp.	7 mL
Fresh sweet basil leaves, stacked, rolled tightly lengthwise, then cut crosswise into very thin slivers (chiffonade)	10	10
Medium tomato, diced	1	1
Rotini pasta (about 6 oz., 170 g)	2¼ cups	550 mL
Salt	1 tbsp.	15 mL
Boiling water	10 cups	2.5 L
Grated Parmesan cheese (optional)	2 tbsp.	30 mL

Preheat lightly sprayed electric grill to medium-high. Poke sausages with fork in several places. Place sausages, green pepper and onion on grill. Cook for about 5 minutes, turning sausages and vegetables several times, until no pink remains in sausage. Cut into thin slices. Dice cooked vegetables.

Lightly sauté garlic in olive oil in small non-stick frying pan for a few seconds. Stir in basil and tomato just until fragrant and warmed. Remove from heat.

Cook pasta and salt in boiling water in large uncovered pot or Dutch oven for 7 to 9 minutes, stirring occasionally, until tender but firm. Rinse with warm water. Drain. Put into large bowl. Pour tomato mixture over pasta. Add sausage and vegetables. Toss together. Sprinkle with Parmesan cheese. Toss. Makes about 7 cups (1.75 L). Serves 4.

1 serving: 393 Calories; 20.2 g Total Fat; 419 mg Sodium; 14 g Protein; 38 g Carbohydrate; 2 g Dietary Fiber

ITALIAN PASTA SKILLET

Sausage, tomatoes and pasta say Italian. Use hot sausage if you like more spice.

Italian sausages, cut into ½ inch (12 mm) pieces	¾ lb.	340 g
Large onion, chopped	1	1
Garlic clove, minced (or ¼ tsp., 1 mL, garlic powder)	1	1
Chopped fresh mushrooms	1 cup	250 mL
Medium green pepper, diced	1	1
Can of diced tomatoes, with juice	28 oz.	796 mL
Tomato (or vegetable) juice	1 cup	250 mL
Water	1 cup	250 mL
Dried sweet basil	2 tsp.	10 mL
Granulated sugar	½ tsp.	2 mL
Dried whole oregano	¼ tsp.	1 mL
Penne pasta (about 6 oz., 170 g), uncooked	2¼ cups	550 mL
Grated Parmesan cheese	2 tbsp.	30 mL
Chopped fresh parsley (or 1½ tsp., 7 mL, flakes)	2 tbsp.	30 mL

Sauté sausage, onion and garlic in large frying pan until onion is soft.

Add mushrooms and green pepper. Sauté until onion and sausage are lightly browned. Drain.

Add next 7 ingredients. Stir together. Cover. Boil gently for 30 to 35 minutes, stirring occasionally, until pasta is tender.

Sprinkle with Parmesan cheese and parsley. Serves 6.

1 serving: 257 Calories; 8.3 g Total Fat; 651 mg Sodium; 12 g Protein; 34 g Carbohydrate; 3 g Dietary Fiber

Pictured on page 72.

Italian

Pasta And Ceci

CHEH-chee is the Italian word for "chick pea."

Small onion, diced	1	1
Garlic clove, minced	1	1
Olive oil	1 tsp.	5 mL
Can of chick peas (garbanzo beans), with liquid	19 oz.	540 mL
Celery rib, diced	1	1
Medium carrot, diced	1	1
Chopped fresh parsley, packed (or 1 tbsp., 15 mL, flakes)	¼ cup	60 mL
Can of roma (plum) tomatoes, with juice, broken up	14 oz.	398 mL
Bay leaf	1	1
Salt	¼ tsp.	1 mL
Ground cumin (optional)	⅛ tsp.	0.5 mL
Dried crushed chilies	⅛ tsp.	0.5 mL
Pepper	⅛ tsp.	0.5 mL
Fettuccine pasta	8 oz.	225 g
Boiling water	8 cups	2 L
Salt	2 tsp.	10 mL
Olive oil	1 tsp.	5 mL
Fettuccine pasta, broken into 1 inch (2.5 cm) lengths, uncooked	2 oz.	57 g

Sauté onion and garlic in first amount of olive oil in large non-stick frying pan until onion is soft. Add chick peas. Bring to a boil. Add celery, carrot and parsley. Reduce heat. Cover. Simmer for 10 minutes until carrot is tender.

Stir in tomatoes with juice. Add bay leaf, first amount of salt, cumin, chilies and pepper. Stir. Bring to a boil. Reduce heat. Simmer, partially covered, for 30 minutes until slightly thickened. Discard bay leaf.

Cook first amount of fettuccine in boiling water and second amount of salt in large uncovered pot or Dutch oven for 8 to 10 minutes, stirring occasionally, until tender but firm. Drain. Return to pot. Pour sauce over top. Toss well. Keep warm.

Heat second amount of olive oil in large non-stick frying pan. Add second amount of fettuccine. Stir-fry for about 3 minutes until golden brown and crisp. Turn out onto paper towel and blot dry. Sprinkle over pasta and sauce. Serve immediately. Serves 4.

1 serving: 482 Calories; 5.4 g Total Fat; 762 mg Sodium; 17 g Protein; 92 g Carbohydrate; 8 g Dietary Fiber

For more even cooking of pasta, wait until the water comes to a full boil before adding the pasta. This also helps prevent sticky pasta.

LAZY RAVIOLI

This cooks and tastes better when baked in a shallow dish.

Lean ground beef	1½ lbs.	680 g
Chopped onion	1½ cups	375 mL
Coarsely chopped fresh mushrooms	1½ cups	375 mL
Garlic clove, minced (or ¼ tsp., 1 mL, garlic powder)	1	1
Can of tomato paste	5½ oz.	156 mL
Can of tomato sauce	7½ oz.	213 mL
Hot water	1 cup	250 mL
Beef bouillon powder	1 tbsp.	15 mL
Parsley flakes	1½ tsp.	7 mL
Dried sweet basil	1½ tsp.	7 mL
Granulated sugar	¾ tsp.	4 mL
Dried whole oregano	¼ tsp.	1 mL
Dried thyme	¼ tsp.	1 mL
Salt	½ tsp.	2 mL
Pepper	¼ tsp.	1 mL
Frozen chopped spinach, cooked and squeezed dry	10 oz.	300 g
Large egg, fork-beaten	1	1
Dry bread crumbs	⅓ cup	75 mL
Parsley flakes	1 tbsp.	15 mL
Grated medium or sharp Cheddar cheese	1 cup	250 mL
Garlic salt	⅛ tsp.	0.5 mL
Ground nutmeg	⅛ tsp.	0.5 mL
Lasagna noodles, broken in half	8	8
Boiling water	16 cups	4 L
Salt	1 tbsp.	15 mL
Cooking oil (optional)		
Grated part-skim mozzarella cheese	1 cup	250 mL

Scramble-fry ground beef, onion, mushrooms and garlic in large non-stick frying pan until no pink remains in beef. Drain. Return to frying pan.

Add next 11 ingredients. Stir. Bring to a boil. Cook, uncovered, until thickened.

Combine next 7 ingredients in small bowl. Mix.

Cook noodles in boiling water, second amount of salt and cooking oil in large uncovered pot or Dutch oven for 14 to 16 minutes, stirring occasionally, until tender but firm. Drain. Rinse with cold water. Drain well.

Arrange layers in ungreased 4 quart (4 L) casserole or small roaster as follows:

1. ½ of beef mixture
2. ½ of noodles
3. All of spinach mixture
4. ½ of noodles
5. ½ of beef mixture
6. All of mozzarella cheese

Cover. Bake in 350°F (175°C) oven for about 45 minutes. Serves 6.

1 serving: *520 Calories; 21.6 g Total Fat; 1159 mg Sodium; 40 g Protein; 42 g Carbohydrate; 5 g Dietary Fiber*

1. Pasta Primavera, page 82
2. Shrimp Frittata, page 31
3. Spaghetti Pie, page 61

Props Courtesy of: Stokes

ITALIAN BEEF CASSEROLE

Prepare in 15 minutes. Ready in less than an hour.

Rotini (or fusilli) pasta, uncooked (about 2 oz., 57 g)	¾ cup	175 mL
Sirloin steak, cut into 2½ x ¼ inch (6.4 x 0.6 cm) strips (or 2 cups, 500 mL, cooked beef, cubed)	1 lb.	454 g
Cooking oil	1 tsp.	5 mL
Small onion, chopped	1	1
Chopped green pepper	½ cup	125 mL
Can of stewed tomatoes, with juice, chopped	19 oz.	540 mL
Can of tomato sauce	7½ oz.	213 mL
All-purpose flour	3 tbsp.	50 mL
Beef bouillon powder	2 tsp.	10 mL
Dried whole oregano	½ tsp.	2 mL
Salt	¼ tsp.	1 mL
Pepper, to taste		

Grated part-skim mozzarella cheese, for garnish

Cook pasta according to package directions. Drain. Keep in cold water.

Sauté beef strips in hot cooking oil in non-stick frying pan for 5 minutes. Add onion and green pepper. Sauté until onion is slightly soft. Add tomatoes.

Combine tomato sauce and flour in small bowl. Stir well. Add to beef mixture. Add bouillon powder, oregano, salt and pepper. Bring to a boil. Heat, stirring often until thickened. Spoon into ungreased 1½ quart (1.5 L) casserole dish. Drain pasta. Combine with beef mixture. Bake, uncovered, in 350°F (175°C) oven for 30 minutes.

Sprinkle individual servings with mozzarella cheese. Serves 4.

1 serving: 632 Calories; 6.1 g Total Fat; 1211 mg Sodium; 28 g Protein; 33 g Carbohydrate; 3 g Dietary Fiber

Pasta is done when tender but still slightly firm — "al dente." When you bite into the pasta it should offer slight resistance but not be soft.

1. Spinach Pasta Roll, page 81
2. Tortellini, page 48
3. Stuffed Manicotti, page 61
4. Jumbo Cheese Shells, page 78

Props Courtesy Of: Stokes

JOHNNY MARZETTI

This is a variation of a recipe that was created by the owner of the Marzetti Restaurant. It was named after the owner's brother.

Large (not jumbo) shell pasta (about 8 oz., 225 g)	3 cups	750 mL
Cooking oil (optional)	1 tbsp.	15 mL
Salt	2 tsp.	10 mL
Water	10 cups	2.5 L
Margarine (or butter)	¼ cup	60 mL
Chopped onion	2 cups	500 mL
Sliced fresh mushrooms	1 cup	250 mL
Chopped celery	½ cup	125 mL
Small green pepper, chopped	1	1
Lean ground beef	1½ lbs.	680 g
Can of condensed tomato soup	10 oz.	284 mL
Can of condensed cream of mushroom soup	10 oz.	284 mL
Can of tomato sauce	7½ oz.	213 mL
Salt	1 tsp.	5 mL
Pepper	¼ tsp.	1 mL
Grated medium Cheddar cheese	1½ cups	375 mL
Grated medium Cheddar cheese	1 cup	250 mL

Cook shells, cooking oil and first amount of salt in boiling water in large uncovered pot or Dutch oven for 5 to 7 minutes, stirring occasionally, until tender but firm. Drain. Rinse with cold water. Drain.

Melt margarine in frying pan. Add next 5 ingredients. Stir-fry until vegetables are soft and no pink remains in beef.

Add both soups. Stir in tomato sauce, second amount of salt and pepper. Turn into small roaster. Add pasta.

Add first amount of cheese. Stir to mix.

Sprinkle with second amount of cheese. Cover. Bake in 350°F (175°C) oven for 30 to 40 minutes until piping hot. Remove cover for last few minutes of baking time to melt cheese. Serves 8.

1 serving: 597 Calories; 35.2 g Total Fat; 1441 mg Sodium; 32 g Protein; 39 g Carbohydrate; 3 g Dietary Fiber

ITALIAN STEAK

Serve with tri-colored rotini.

Round steak	1½ lbs.	680 g
MARINADE		
Dry white (or alcohol-free) wine	½ cup	125 mL
Freshly ground pepper, to taste		
Sprigs of fresh rosemary, chopped	2	2
Chopped fresh sweet basil	2 tbsp.	30 mL
Bay leaf	1	1
SAUCE		
Can of tomato sauce	7½ oz.	213 mL
Chopped onion	¼ cup	60 mL
Minced garlic	½ tsp.	2 mL
Chopped fresh sweet basil	1 tbsp.	15 mL
Dried whole oregano	½ tsp.	2 mL

Pound steak with meat mallet. Place in shallow dish or resealable plastic bag.

Marinade: Combine wine, pepper, rosemary, basil and bay leaf in small bowl. Pour over steak. Turn to coat. Cover or seal. Marinate in refrigerator overnight, turning several times. Remove steak, straining and reserving marinade. Place on rack in broiler pan. Broil for about 8 minutes per side for rare or to desired doneness. Slice thinly across grain.

Sauce: Combine all 5 ingredients and reserved marinade in small saucepan. Bring to a boil. Reduce heat. Cover. Simmer for 5 to 10 minutes. Pour over steak. Makes 1 cup (250 mL) sauce. Serves 6.

1 serving: 145 Calories; 2.8 g Total Fat; 270 mg Sodium; 22 g Protein; 4 g Carbohydrate; 1 g Dietary Fiber

Pictured on page 71.

PASTA ITALIA

Allow 1½ hours to prepare and cook.

Sirloin steak, cut into ¾ inch (2 cm) cubes	1 lb.	454 g
Garlic cloves, minced	3	3
Olive oil	1 tsp.	5 mL
Can of crushed tomatoes	14 oz.	398 mL
Water	¾ cup	175 mL
Medium red pepper, diced	1	1
Medium yellow pepper, diced	1	1
Medium zucchini, with peel, diced	1	1
Olive oil	1 tsp.	5 mL
Dried crushed chilies	¼ tsp.	1 mL
Chopped fresh sweet basil	2 tbsp.	30 mL
Dried whole oregano	¾ tsp.	4 mL
Salt	½ tsp.	2 mL
Pitted ripe olives	18	18
Can of artichoke hearts, drained and quartered	14 oz.	398 mL
Fusilli pasta, uncooked (8 oz., 250 g)	2⅔ cups	650 mL

Stir-fry beef and garlic in first amount of olive oil in non-stick frying pan or wok for 3 to 5 minutes on medium-high. Add tomatoes and water. Reduce heat. Cover. Simmer for 45 to 60 minutes.

Stir-fry both peppers and zucchini in second amount of olive oil in separate non-stick frying pan or wok on medium-high until juices are released. Add chilies, basil, oregano and salt. Reduce heat. Simmer for 5 minutes. Pour over beef mixture. Add olives and artichoke hearts. Mix well. Keep warm.

Prepare pasta according to package directions. Drain. Serve beef and vegetables on pasta. Serves 6.

1 serving: 317 Calories; 6.2 g Total Fat; 522 mg Sodium; 23 g Protein; 43 g Carbohydrate; 3 g Dietary Fiber

OSSO BUCO

A well-known Italian meal that is accompanied by Risotto Milanese, page 104. Gravy is excellent.

All-purpose flour	1 cup	250 mL
Salt	2 tsp.	10 mL
Pepper	½ tsp.	2 mL
Veal shanks, cut into 2 inch (5 cm) lengths	3	3
Margarine (butter browns too fast)	¼ cup	60 mL
Large onions, cut into wedges or chunks	3	3
Medium carrots, cut bite size	10	10
Sliced celery	1½ cups	375 mL
Parsley flakes	1 tbsp.	15 mL
Dry white (or alcohol-free) wine	1 cup	250 mL
Water	2 cups	500 mL
Beef bouillon cubes (⅕ oz., 6 g, each)	3	3
Cans of tomato sauce (7½ oz., 213 mL, each)	2	2
Lemon juice	1 tbsp.	15 mL

Combine flour, salt and pepper in plastic or paper bag. Shake well.

Add veal, a few pieces at a time. Shake to coat.

Melt margarine in frying pan. Brown veal, adding more margarine if needed.

Put onion, carrot, celery and parsley into bottom of roaster. Place veal on vegetables.

Pour wine into frying pan. Stir to loosen any stuck bits of veal. Boil until reduced to about ¼ of original amount.

Add water and bouillon cubes. Stir to dissolve cubes. Stir in tomato sauce and lemon juice. Pour over contents in roaster. Cover. Bake in 325°F (160°C) oven for about 2 hours until veal is fork-tender. Add more liquid if too dry. Gravy should be quite thick when done. If too thin, remove veal and vegetables. Keep warm. Boil sauce, uncovered, until thickened. Serves 8.

1 serving: 363 Calories; 11.4 g Total Fat; 1600 mg Sodium; 27 g Protein; 34 g Carbohydrate; 5 g Dietary Fiber

STEAK 'N' PENNE

A hearty meal. Great served with a salad and bun. Only ten minutes preparation time.

Lean boneless beef steak (such as top round), cut into ¾ inch (2 cm) cubes	1 lb.	454 g
Cooking oil	1 tsp.	5 mL
Chopped onion	1½ cups	375 mL
Garlic clove, minced (optional)	1	1
Can of condensed beef consommé	10 oz.	284 mL
Bay leaf	1	1
Pepper	¼ tsp.	1 mL
Dried thyme	¼ tsp.	1 mL
Parsley flakes	1 tbsp.	15 mL
Diced carrot	1½ cups	375 mL
Tomato (or vegetable) juice	2 cups	500 mL
Penne pasta, uncooked (8 oz., 225 g)	2⅔ cups	650 mL
Medium tomatoes, diced	2	2

Sauté beef in cooking oil in large non-stick frying pan until browned. Add onion and garlic. Sauté until onion is soft.

Add next 6 ingredients. Stir. Bring to a boil. Reduce heat. Cover. Simmer for 30 minutes. Discard bay leaf.

Stir in tomato juice. Bring to a boil. Add pasta. Reduce heat. Cover. Simmer for 10 minutes. Remove cover. Cook until liquid is slightly evaporated and pasta is tender. Add tomato. Stir to heat through. Serves 6.

1 serving: 287 Calories; 3.4 g Total Fat; 606 mg Sodium; 23 g Protein; 41 g Carbohydrate; 3 g Dietary Fiber

PENNE WITH WINE VEGETABLE SAUCE

Lots of chopping but ready in 40 minutes.

Penne pasta, uncooked (8 oz., 225 g)	2⅔ cups	650 mL
Margarine (or butter)	2 tbsp.	30 mL
All-purpose flour	3 tbsp.	50 mL
Skim evaporated milk	1 cup	250 mL
Lean ground beef	1 lb.	454 g
Large onion, cut into slivers	1	1
Garlic cloves, minced	4	4
Sliced fresh mushrooms	3 cups	750 mL
Medium red pepper, cut into 2 inch (5 cm) strips	1	1
Dry white (or alcohol-free) wine	1 cup	250 mL
Can of diced tomatoes, with juice	28 oz.	796 mL
Finely chopped fresh sweet basil	¼ cup	60 mL

Cook pasta according to package directions. Drain. Rinse with warm water. Drain.

Melt margarine in small saucepan. Stir in flour. Gradually whisk in evaporated milk until sauce is smooth and bubbling. Remove from heat. Cover. Set aside.

Scramble-fry ground beef in large saucepan until no pink remains. Drain. Add onion and garlic. Sauté until onion is soft. Add mushrooms and red pepper. Sauté for 5 minutes until vegetables release their juices and mixture is bubbling.

Add wine and tomatoes with juice. Bring to a boil. Stir in milk mixture and basil. Add pasta. Stir. Serves 6.

1 serving: 435 Calories; 11.5 g Total Fat; 354 mg Sodium; 25 g Protein; 51 g Carbohydrate; 3 g Dietary Fiber

Spaghetti And Meatballs

Everyone knows this pasta dish. Meatballs are cooked in the sauce.

MEATBALLS

Lean ground beef	1 lb.	454 g
Chopped onion	½ cup	125 mL
Dry bread crumbs	½ cup	125 mL
Grated Parmesan cheese	¼ cup	60 mL
Salt	1 tsp.	5 mL
Pepper	¼ tsp.	1 mL
Large eggs	2	2

SPAGHETTI SAUCE

Chopped onion	1 cup	250 mL
Can of diced tomatoes, with juice	28 oz.	796 mL
Can of tomato paste	5½ oz.	156 mL
Can of sliced mushrooms, drained	10 oz.	284 mL
Granulated sugar	2 tsp.	10 mL
Parsley flakes	1 tsp.	5 mL
Salt	1 tsp.	5 mL
Pepper	¼ tsp.	1 mL
Bay leaf	1	1
Spaghetti	8 oz.	225 g
Cooking oil (optional)	1 tbsp.	15 mL
Salt	2 tsp.	10 mL
Water	10 cups	2.5 L
Grated Parmesan cheese	½ cup	125 mL

Meatballs: Combine all 7 ingredients in medium bowl. Mix well. Shape into about 28 meatballs. Chill until ready to use.

Spaghetti Sauce: Combine all 9 ingredients in large saucepan. Mix. Simmer, uncovered, for 20 minutes, stirring occasionally. Add meatballs. Cover. Simmer for 20 to 25 minutes. Discard bay leaf.

Cook spaghetti, cooking oil and salt in boiling water in large uncovered pot or Dutch oven for 11 to 13 minutes, stirring occasionally, until tender but firm. Drain. Turn spaghetti out onto warm platter or 4 plates.

Spoon meatballs and sauce over center of spaghetti. Sprinkle heavily with Parmesan cheese. Serves 4.

1 serving: 779 Calories; 28.3 g Total Fat; 2452 mg Sodium; 47 g Protein; 85 g Carbohydrate; 8 g Dietary Fiber

Penne With Tomato And Beef

Prepare the vegetables while the pasta is cooking.

Penne (or rigatoni) pasta (about 6 oz., 170 g), uncooked	2 cups	500 mL
Top round steak, cut into ⅛ inch (3 mm) strips	1 lb.	454 g
Garlic cloves, minced	2	2
Finely chopped onion	2 tbsp.	30 mL
Chopped fresh sweet basil	2 tbsp.	30 mL
Dried thyme	1 tsp.	5 mL
Dried whole oregano	1 tsp.	5 mL
Can of tomato paste	5½ oz.	156 mL
Can of tomatoes, with juice, puréed	19 oz.	540 mL
Medium green pepper, slivered	1	1

Cook pasta according to package directions. Drain. Rinse with water. Drain.

Heat non-stick frying pan or wok until hot. Stir-fry beef strips for 1 to 2 minutes. Add garlic, onion, basil, thyme and oregano. Stir-fry for 2 minutes until no pink remains in beef. Stir in tomato paste and puréed tomato. Mix well. Reduce heat. Cover. Simmer for 15 minutes. Add green pepper. Cover. Simmer for about 5 minutes until beef is tender. Add pasta. Stir until coated. Serves 6.

1 serving: 269 Calories; 3.7 g Total Fat; 73 mg Sodium; 22 g Protein; 39 g Carbohydrate; 5 g Dietary Fiber

SPINACH-STUFFED SHELLS

Cooked in a zesty meat sauce.

MEAT SAUCE

Lean ground beef	½ lb.	225 g
Chopped onion	2 tbsp.	30 mL
Cooking oil	2 tsp.	10 mL
Can of tomato paste	5½ oz.	156 mL
Water	1¼ cups	300 mL
Salt	1 tsp.	5 mL
Parsley flakes	¼ tsp.	1 mL
Dried whole oregano	⅛ tsp.	0.5 mL
Garlic powder	⅛ tsp.	0.5 mL
Dried sweet basil	⅛ tsp.	0.5 mL
Jumbo (very large) shell pasta	20	20
Boiling water	10 cups	2.5 L
Cooking oil (optional)	1 tbsp.	15 mL
Salt	2 tsp.	10 mL

SPINACH FILLING

Frozen chopped spinach, thawed and squeezed dry	10 oz.	300 g
Creamed cottage cheese	1 cup	250 mL
Grated mozzarella cheese	1 cup	250 mL
Grated Parmesan cheese	2 tbsp.	30 mL

Meat Sauce: Scramble-fry ground beef and onion in first amount of cooking oil until no pink remains in beef.

Add next 7 ingredients. Mix. Remove from heat.

Cook pasta in boiling water, second amounts of cooking oil and salt in large uncovered pot or Dutch oven for 12 to 15 minutes, stirring occasionally, until tender but firm. Drain. Rinse with cold water. Drain well.

Spinach filling: Mix all 4 ingredients. Stuff pasta using 2 rounded spoonfuls each. Put ½ of meat sauce in 9 x 9 inch (22 x 22 cm) pan. Lay pasta on top. Spoon on second ½ of sauce. Cover. Bake in 350°F (175°C) oven for 30 to 40 minutes until bubbly hot. Makes 20 stuffed shells.

1 stuffed shell: 104 Calories; 5.1 g Total Fat; 246 mg Sodium; 7 g Protein; 8 g Carbohydrate; 1 g Dietary Fiber

VEAL MARSALA

Steak in wine and mushroom mixture. So tender and full of flavor.

Margarine (butter browns too fast)	2 tbsp.	30 mL
Veal sirloin steak	5 lbs.	2.3 kg
All-purpose flour	⅔ cup	150 mL
Salt, sprinkle		
Pepper, sprinkle		
Marsala wine or sherry (or alcohol-free wine or sherry)	1 cup	250 mL
Water	1 cup	250 mL
Beef bouillon powder	2 tsp.	10 mL
Cans of sliced mushrooms, (10 oz., 284 mL, each), drained	2	2

Melt margarine in frying pan.

Dredge steak in flour. Add to frying pan. Brown on both sides.

Remove steaks to platter. Sprinkle with salt and pepper.

Add marsala and water to same frying pan. Stir to loosen any stuck bits of steak. Add bouillon powder and mushrooms. Stir. Return steaks, a few at a time, to frying pan. Simmer for 3 minutes, turning once. Transfer steaks only to platter in warm oven. Repeat with remaining steaks. Pour sauce over steaks on platter. Serves 8.

1 serving: 306 Calories; 8.2 g Total Fat; 352 mg Sodium; 41 g Protein; 9 g Carbohydrate; trace Dietary Fiber

STUFFED MANICOTTI

Assemble in the morning. Bake in the afternoon.

Lean ground beef	1 lb.	454 g
Dried whole oregano	2 tsp.	10 mL
Granulated sugar	1 tsp.	5 mL
Can of tomato sauce	14 oz.	398 mL
Can of stewed tomatoes, with juice, chopped	28 oz.	796 mL
Part-skim ricotta cheese	2 cups	500 mL
Grated Parmesan cheese	⅓ cup	75 mL
Grated part-skim mozzarella cheese	¾ cup	175 mL
Large eggs	2	2
Chopped fresh spinach	2¼ cups	550 mL
Manicotti pasta shells, uncooked	14	14
Grated part-skim mozzarella cheese	1 cup	250 mL

Scramble-fry ground beef in medium saucepan until no pink remains. Drain. Stir in oregano, sugar, tomato sauce and tomatoes with juice. Reduce heat. Cover. Simmer for 10 minutes.

Combine 3 cheeses with eggs and spinach. Mix well. Stuff manicotti shells with cheese mixture. Spread 1 cup (250 mL) meat sauce in bottom of ungreased 9 x 13 inch (22 x 33 cm) baking pan. Arrange stuffed shells in single layer on top. Pour remaining sauce over all. Cover tightly with foil. Bake in 350°F (175°C) oven for 1¼ hours.

Sprinkle with second amount of mozzarella cheese. Bake, uncovered, 5 to 8 minutes until cheese is melted. Makes 14 stuffed manicotti plus 5 cups (1.25 L) sauce.

1 manicotti (with 2 tbsp., 10 mL, sauce): 222 Calories; 9.5 g Total Fat; 510 mg Sodium; 17.8 g Protein; 17 g Carbohydrate; 1 g Dietary Fiber

Pictured on page 54.

SPAGHETTI PIE

From start to finish in less than 45 minutes.

Spaghetti, uncooked	8 oz.	225 g
Dried sweet basil, crumbled	1 tsp.	5 mL
Lean ground beef	1 lb.	454 g
Tomato sauce	14 oz.	398 mL
Garlic clove, minced	1	1
Dried whole oregano	1 tsp.	5 mL
Chopped sun-dried tomatoes, softened in boiling water for 5 minutes before chopping	¼ cup	60 mL
Jar of marinated artichoke hearts, drained and rinsed	6 oz.	170 mL
Grated part-skim mozzarella cheese	1 cup	250 mL

Cook pasta according to package directions. Drain. Rinse with cold water. Drain well.

Toss pasta with basil. Press firmly against bottom and sides of lightly sprayed 2½ quart (2.5 L) casserole or deep 10 inch (25 cm) pie plate to form a thick "crust."

Scramble-fry ground beef in non-stick frying pan. Drain. Add tomato sauce, garlic, oregano and sun-dried tomato. Reduce heat. Cover. Simmer for 6 minutes, stirring occasionally. Pour mixture into spaghetti crust.

Arrange artichoke hearts in sauce mixture. Bake, uncovered, in 350°F (175°C) oven for 15 to 20 minutes.

Sprinkle with cheese. Bake for 5 minutes until cheese is melted. Cuts into 6 wedges.

1 wedge: 362 Calories; 10.4 g Total Fat; 571 mg Sodium; 26 g Protein; 41 g Carbohydrate; 2 g Dietary Fiber

Pictured on page 53.

GROUND BEEF AND SPAGHETTI PIE

Many ingredients but worth every one. Takes about 35 minutes preparation time to get to the oven stage.

Spaghetti	6 oz.	170 g
Boiling water	6 cups	1.5 L
Salt	1½ tsp.	7 mL
Lean ground beef	¾ lb.	340 g
Chopped onion	1 cup	250 mL
Large garlic clove, minced	1	1
All-purpose flour	1½ tbsp.	25 mL
Granulated sugar	½ tsp.	2 mL
Ground cloves, sprinkle (optional)		
Ground nutmeg, sprinkle (optional)		
Can of stewed tomatoes, processed	14 oz.	398 mL
Frozen mixed vegetables	1 cup	250 mL
Frozen egg product, thawed	8 oz.	227 mL
Fine dry bread crumbs	¼ cup	60 mL
Beef bouillon powder	1 tsp.	5 mL
Skim milk	2 cups	500 mL
All-purpose flour	2 tbsp.	30 mL
Light salad dressing (or mayonnaise)	1 tbsp.	15 mL
Grated light Cheddar cheese	½ cup	125 mL
Grated part-skim mozzarella cheese	½ cup	125 mL

Paprika, sprinkle
Chopped fresh parsley, for garnish

Cook pasta in boiling water and salt in large saucepan for 8 minutes, stirring occasionally, until tender but firm. Drain. Rinse with warm water. Drain.

Scramble-fry ground beef, onion and garlic in large non-stick frying pan until no pink remains in beef. Drain. Sprinkle with first amount of flour. Mix well. Stir in sugar, cloves, nutmeg, tomatoes and vegetables. Bring to a boil. Reduce heat. Simmer, uncovered, for 15 minutes.

Place ½ of egg product in medium bowl. Add ground beef mixture. Add bread crumbs and bouillon powder. Mix well. Pour into lightly sprayed deep 10 inch (25 cm) glass pie plate. Spread pasta evenly on top.

Gradually whisk milk into second amount of flour in medium saucepan until smooth. Cook, whisking often, until boiling and thickened. Remove from heat. Stir in salad dressing, Cheddar cheese and mozzarella cheese until melted. Stir in remaining ½ of egg product. Pour mixture evenly over pasta.

Sprinkle with paprika and parsley. Bake, uncovered, in 350°F (175°C) oven for 50 minutes until center is set and top is golden. Let stand for 10 minutes before cutting. Cuts into 8 wedges.

1 wedge: *294 Calories; 7.8 g Total Fat; 448 mg Sodium; 22 g Protein; 34 g Carbohydrate; 2 g Dietary Fiber*

If your cheese is getting old, grate and freeze in sealable plastic bags. It can then be used for nachos, casseroles, sprinkled on pasta or in grilled cheese sandwiches.

CHICKEN PASTA CASSEROLE

Good, basic casserole for a rainy day.

Lean ground chicken	1 lb.	454 g
Garlic clove, minced	1	1
Medium onion, chopped	1	1
Salt	½ tsp.	2 mL
Pepper, sprinkle		
Celery rib, chopped	1	1
Medium carrot, grated	1	1
All-purpose flour	2 tbsp.	30 mL
Frozen peas	1 cup	250 mL
Elbow macaroni, uncooked (4 oz., 113 g)	1 cup	250 mL
Water	1 cup	250 mL
Chicken bouillon powder	2 tsp.	10 mL
Skim evaporated milk	¾ cup	175 mL
Coarsely crushed corn flakes cereal	¼ cup	60 mL
Grated light Swiss cheese	¼ cup	60 mL

Scramble-fry chicken with garlic and onion in medium non-stick frying pan for 5 minutes. Sprinkle with salt and pepper. Add celery, carrot and flour. Stir together. Cook for about 1 minute.

Place ½ of chicken mixture in bottom of greased 2 quart (2 L) casserole. Scatter with peas and macaroni.

Heat water, bouillon powder and evaporated milk in small saucepan until almost boiling. Pour ½ of sauce over macaroni. Cover with remaining chicken mixture. Pour remaining sauce over all. Cover. Bake in 350°F (175°C) oven for 45 minutes until pasta is cooked and liquid is mostly absorbed.

Combine cereal and cheese in small bowl. Sprinkle over casserole. Bake, uncovered, in 350°F (175°C) oven for 10 to 15 minutes until topping is browned. Serves 4.

1 serving: 382 Calories; 5.4 g Total Fat; 967 mg Sodium; 36 g Protein; 46 g Carbohydrate; 4 g Dietary Fiber

CHICKEN AND ORZO

Very easy. Only 20 minutes preparation time.

Boneless, skinless chicken breast halves (about 2), sliced paper-thin	½ lb.	225 g
Garlic cloves, minced	2	2
Olive oil	1 tsp.	5 mL
Can of condensed chicken broth	10 oz.	284 mL
Water	1 cup	250 mL
Low-sodium soy sauce	1 tbsp.	15 mL
Medium carrot, cut julienne	1	1
Orzo pasta, uncooked	1 cup	250 mL
Small zucchini, cut julienne	1	1
Medium red pepper, quartered lengthwise and sliced crosswise	1	1

Stir-fry chicken and garlic in olive oil in large non-stick frying pan or wok for 5 minutes until chicken is almost cooked.

Add next 5 ingredients. Reduce heat. Cover. Simmer for 10 minutes.

Stir in zucchini and red pepper. Cover. Cook for 5 minutes until pasta is tender and liquid is absorbed. Serves 4.

1 serving: 351 Calories; 3.7 g Total Fat; 749 mg Sodium; 26 g Protein; 52 g Carbohydrate; 3 g Dietary Fiber

Roasted Chicken And Vegetables

Chicken and vegetables are served over penne pasta. Thickening the sauce is optional.

Boneless, skinless chicken breast halves (about 4), cut into ¼ inch (6 mm) slivers	1 lb.	454 g
Non-fat Italian dressing	½ cup	125 mL
Non-fat Italian dressing	½ cup	125 mL
Garlic clove, minced	1	1
Dried sweet basil	¼ tsp.	1 mL
Dried rosemary, crushed	⅛ tsp.	0.5 mL
Large onion, cut into wedges	1	1
Small green or red peppers, cut into ½ inch (12 mm) slivers	2	2
Medium zucchini, with peel, sliced ¼ inch (6 mm) thick	1	1
Olive oil	2 tsp.	10 mL
Medium roma (plum) tomatoes, cut into ½ inch (12 mm) slices	3	3
Cornstarch (optional)	2 tsp.	10 mL
Dry white wine (or water), optional	1 tbsp.	15 mL
Penne pasta (about 8 oz., 225 g)	2⅔ cups	650 mL
Boiling water	12 cups	3 L
Salt	1 tbsp.	15 mL

Combine chicken and first amount of dressing. Set aside.

Combine second amount of dressing, garlic, basil and rosemary in large bowl. Add onion, green pepper and zucchini. Stir to lightly coat. Add chicken mixture. Mix well. Spread evenly on baking sheet greased with olive oil. Bake on top rack in 450°F (230°C) oven for 10 minutes. Add tomato. Bake for 5 to 10 minutes until no pink remains in chicken and vegetables are tender-crisp. Turn into serving bowl.

Combine cornstarch and wine in small saucepan. Add liquid from cooked chicken and vegetables. Heat and stir until boiling and thickened. Add to chicken and vegetables. Stir.

Cook pasta in boiling water and salt in large uncovered pot or Dutch oven for 8 to 10 minutes, stirring occasionally, until tender but firm. Drain. Rinse with warm water. Drain. Toss with chicken mixture. Makes 6½ cups (1.6 L) without pasta. Serves 4.

1 serving: 446 Calories; 5.2 g Total Fat; 798 mg Sodium; 36 g Protein; 63 g Carbohydrate; 4 g Dietary Fiber

STUFFED TURKEY SCALLOPINI

What a wonderful stuffing surprise inside!

Lean prosciutto (or ham), chopped	4 oz.	113 g
Grated part-skim mozzarella cheese	½ cup	125 mL
Garlic clove, minced	1	1
Chopped fresh parsley	1 tbsp.	15 mL
Chopped fresh sweet basil	1 tbsp.	15 mL
Thin turkey scallopini	1 lb.	454 g
Can of diced tomatoes, with juice	28 oz.	796 mL
Granulated sugar	1 tsp.	5 mL
Dried sweet basil	1 tsp.	5 mL
Dried whole oregano	½ tsp.	2 mL
Pepper	¼ tsp.	1 mL
Cornstarch	1 tbsp.	15 mL
Water	1 tbsp.	15 mL
Spaghetti (or vermicelli)	8 oz.	225 g

Combine first 5 ingredients in small bowl.

Pound out scallopini with flat side of mallet to about ¼ inch (6 mm) thickness. Cut into 8 pieces. Place about 3 tbsp. (50 mL) prosciutto mixture on narrow end of each scallopini. Roll up, tucking in sides. Secure with wooden picks. Lightly grease non-stick frying pan. Brown on all sides until golden.

Add tomatoes with juice to rolls. Stir in sugar, basil, oregano and pepper. Simmer for 30 minutes. Remove rolls to plate. Keep warm.

Mix cornstarch and water in small cup. Stir into tomato mixture until slightly thickened.

Cook pasta according to package directions. Drain. Toss with 1 cup (250 mL) sauce. Serve remaining sauce over rolls. Serves 4.

1 serving: 518 Calories; 11.2 g Total Fat; 968 mg Sodium; 48 g Protein; 56 g Carbohydrate; 3 g Dietary Fiber

Pictured on page 71.

CHICKEN SCALLOPINI

A takeoff from veal scallopini.

Boneless, skinless chicken breast halves (about 4 oz., 113 g, each)	8	8
All-purpose flour	½ cup	125 mL
Margarine (not butter)	2 tbsp.	30 mL
Garlic powder	⅛ tsp.	0.5 mL
Chicken bouillon powder	1 tsp.	5 mL
Marsala (or alcohol-free) wine	3 tbsp.	50 mL
Dry white (or alcohol-free) wine	3 tbsp.	50 mL
Water	1 cup	250 mL
Chicken bouillon powder	1 tbsp.	15 mL
Cornstarch	2 tbsp.	30 mL
Prosciutto (or ham) slices	8	8
Mozzarella cheese slices	8	8

Gently pound chicken breasts with mallet until flattened. Dip into flour to coat.

Combine margarine, garlic and boillion powders. Brown chicken on both sides, in two batches, until no longer pink. Arrange on broiler pan.

Measure next 5 ingredients into small saucepan. Mix well. Heat and stir on medium until boiling and thickened. Makes 1 cup (250 mL).

Lay slices of ham and cheese over each chicken breast. Broil close to heat until cheese is melted and browned. Spoon on sauce. Serves 8.

1 serving: 217 Calories; 9 g Total Fat; 794 mg Sodium; 22 g Protein; 9 g Carbohydrate; trace Dietary Fiber

CHICKEN CACCIATORE

Reddish in color. Tomato adds its own flavor.
Excellent choice.

Chopped onion	1½ cups	375 mL
Chicken parts, skin removed	3 lbs.	1.4 kg
Can of diced tomatoes, with juice	14 oz.	398 mL
Can of tomato paste	5½ oz.	156 mL
Can of mushroom pieces, drained	10 oz.	284 mL
Bay leaf	1	1
Salt	1 tsp.	5 mL
Pepper	¼ tsp.	1 mL
Garlic powder	¼ tsp.	1 mL
Dried whole oregano	1 tsp.	5 mL
Dried sweet basil	½ tsp.	2 mL
Dry white (or alcohol-free) wine	¼ cup	60 mL
Liquid gravy browner	½ tsp.	2 mL
Granulated sugar	1 tsp.	5 mL

Place onion and chicken in 3½ quart (3.5 L) slow cooker.

Combine next 12 ingredients in medium bowl. Stir. Pour over chicken. Cover. Cook on Low for 6 to 8 hours or on High for 3 to 4 hours. Discard bay leaf. Serves 4.

1 serving: 306 Calories; 5.7 g Total Fat; 1178 mg Sodium; 40 g Protein; 22 g Carbohydrate; 5 g Dietary Fiber

CHICKEN AND ASPARAGUS PASTA

Leeks look like giant scallions. The leek is related to onion and garlic, although its aroma and flavor are milder.

Ditali pasta (about 10 oz., 285 g)	2½ cups	625 mL
Boiling water	10 cups	2.5 L
Salt	2½ tsp.	12 mL

Fresh asparagus	1 lb.	454 g
Water	¾ cup	175 mL
Dry white (or alcohol-free) wine	¼ cup	60 mL
Chicken bouillon powder	2 tsp.	10 mL
Medium leek, thinly sliced (see Tip, page 84)	1	1
Garlic cloves, minced	2	2
Skim evaporated milk	¾ cup	175 mL
All-purpose flour	2 tbsp.	30 mL
Diced cooked chicken	2 cups	500 mL
Grated light Parmesan cheese	2 tbsp.	30 mL

Cook pasta in boiling water and salt in large uncovered pot or Dutch oven for 9 to 11 minutes, stirring occasionally, until tender but firm. Drain.

Reserve eight 4 inch (10 cm) asparagus tips for top of casserole. Cut remaining asparagus into 1 inch (2.5 cm) lengths. Heat water, wine and bouillon powder in medium saucepan until boiling. Add leek, asparagus pieces and garlic. Stir. Reduce heat. Cover. Simmer for 10 minutes. Remove cover. Lay reserved tips on top. Cover. Cook for 5 minutes until tips are bright green. Remove tips carefully with slotted spoon and set aside.

Stir evaporated milk and flour together in small bowl until smooth. Stir into asparagus mixture. Heat and stir until boiling and thickened. Stir in chicken. Add pasta. Mix. Turn into greased 3 quart (3 L) casserole. Arrange cooked asparagus tips over top in pinwheel design. Sprinkle with Parmesan cheese. Cover. Bake in 350°F (175°C) oven for 25 to 30 minutes until hot and bubbling. Serves 6.

1 serving: 341 Calories; 3.3 g Total Fat; 340 mg Sodium; 28 g Protein; 48 g Carbohydrate; 3 g Dietary Fiber

Variation: Omit Parmesan cheese. Add ½ cup (125 mL) grated light Cheddar cheese.

ANGEL CHICKEN

Cook the pasta during the second baking time of the vegetables.

Can of stewed tomatoes, with juice, chopped	14 oz.	398 mL
Garlic clove, crushed	1	1
Diced zucchini	2 cups	500 mL
Medium yellow pepper, diced	1	1
Dried sweet basil	2 tsp.	10 mL
Granulated sugar	¼ tsp.	1 mL
Boneless, skinless chicken breast halves (about 4 oz., 113 g, each)	4	4
Grated part-skim mozzarella cheese	1 cup	250 mL
Angel hair pasta	8 oz.	225 g
Salt (optional)	1 tsp.	5 mL
Water	8 cups	2 L
Freshly grated Parmesan cheese	1 tbsp.	15 mL

Mix tomatoes with garlic in small bowl. Pour into ungreased 2 quart (2 L) casserole.

Layer zucchini, yellow pepper, basil and sugar on tomato mixture. Lay chicken on vegetable mixture. Spoon some of tomato mixture over chicken. Bake, uncovered, in 350°F (175°C) oven for 1 hour. Sprinkle with cheese. Bake, uncovered, for about 10 minutes, until cheese is melted. Carefully remove chicken to bowl. Set aside.

Cook pasta and salt in boiling water in large uncovered pot or Dutch oven for 7 to 9 minutes, stirring occasionally, until tender but firm. Drain. Rinse. Drain again. Place on large serving platter. Pour tomato mixture over pasta. Toss lightly to combine. Lay chicken on pasta.

Sprinkle with Parmesan cheese. Serves 4.

1 serving: 468 Calories; 7.9 g Total Fat; 522 mg Sodium; 44 g Protein; 54 g Carbohydrate; 4 g Dietary Fiber

CHICKEN FAGIOLI STEW

Fawj-OH-lee is the Italian word for "beans." Serve in shallow bowls with fresh, crusty bread.

Boneless, skinless chicken breast halves (about 4)	1 lb.	454 g
Low-fat Italian dressing	¼ cup	60 mL
Large onion, coarsely chopped	1	1
Garlic clove, crushed	1	1
Sliced celery, cut into ¼ inch (6 mm) pieces	1 cup	250 mL
Sliced carrot, cut into ¼ inch (6 mm) coins	1 cup	250 mL
Medium potatoes, peeled and cut into 1½ inch (3.8 cm) cubes	3	3
Can of condensed chicken broth	10 oz.	284 mL
Dried rosemary, crushed	1 tsp.	5 mL
Chopped fresh sweet basil	¼ cup	60 ml
Sun-dried tomato halves, softened in boiling water for 10 minutes, finely chopped	6	6
Can of cannellini (white kidney) beans, drained and rinsed	19 oz.	540 mL

Cut chicken breasts into 1 inch (2.5 cm) chunks. Combine with dressing in medium bowl. Set aside.

Lightly grease non-stick frying pan or wok. Sauté onion and garlic for 2 minutes. Add chicken mixture. Sauté for 5 minutes.

Add celery, carrot, potato, broth, rosemary, basil and tomato. Reduce heat. Cover. Simmer for 40 minutes until vegetables are tender. Stir in beans. Simmer, uncovered, until hot. Serves 6.

1 serving: 215 Calories; 2.5 g Total Fat; 653 mg Sodium; 26 g Protein; 23 g Carbohydrate; 5 g Dietary Fiber

Pictured on page 72.

CHICKEN TETRAZZINI

Creamy chicken over fine noodles with a crispy-brown cheese topping.

Margarine (or butter)	3 tbsp.	50 mL
Chopped onion	1 cup	250 mL
Sliced fresh mushrooms	2 cups	500 mL
All-purpose flour	3 tbsp.	50 mL
Salt	½ tsp.	2 mL
Pepper	⅛ tsp.	0.5 mL
Ground nutmeg, just a pinch		
Chicken bouillon powder	1 tbsp.	15 mL
Water	2 cups	500 mL
Skim evaporated milk	1 cup	250 mL
Sherry (or alcohol-free sherry)	2 tbsp.	30 mL
Cubed cooked chicken	3 cups	750 mL
Vermicelli pasta, broken up	8 oz.	225 g
Boiling water	12 cups	3 L
Cooking oil (optional)	1 tbsp.	15 mL
Salt (optional)	1 tbsp.	15 mL
Grated Parmesan cheese	½ cup	125 mL

Melt margarine in frying pan. Add onion. Sauté for 3 to 4 minutes.

Add mushrooms. Sauté until onion is soft.

Mix in flour, first amount of salt, pepper, nutmeg and bouillon powder. Stir in water and milk until boiling and thickened.

Add sherry and chicken. Heat through.

In large uncovered pot or Dutch oven cook vermicelli in boiling water, cooking oil and second amount of salt for 4 to 6 minutes, stirring occasionally, until tender but firm. Drain. Add to chicken mixture. Turn into 3 quart (3 L) casserole.

Sprinkle with Parmesan cheese. Bake, uncovered, in 350°F (175°C) oven for about 20 minutes until browned and hot. Serves 6.

1 serving: 463 Calories; 22.6 g Total Fat; 1079 mg Sodium; 24 g Protein; 40 g Carbohydrate; 2 g Dietary Fiber

ZUCCHINI PESTO SAUTÉ

Beautiful green sauce that coats the pasta nicely.

Medium zucchini, with peel, grated	4	4
Salt	2 tsp.	10 mL
Basil Pesto, page 91 (or commercial)	2 tbsp.	30 mL
Garlic cloves, minced	3	3
Spaghettini, broken into thirds	8 oz.	225 g
Boiling water	8 cups	2 L
Olive oil	2 tsp.	10 mL
Freshly ground pepper, sprinkle		
Grated light Parmesan cheese	2 tbsp.	30 mL

Toss zucchini and salt in large colander set in sink or large bowl to catch drips. Let stand for 15 minutes. Drain liquid by squeezing or by pushing through cheesecloth. Place zucchini in medium bowl. Combine well with pesto and garlic.

Cook pasta in boiling water in large uncovered pot or Dutch oven for 5 to 6 minutes, stirring occasionally, until tender but firm. Drain. Rinse with hot water. Drain. Place in pasta bowl.

Heat large non-stick frying pan or wok until hot. Sauté ½ of zucchini mixture in 1 tsp. (5 mL) olive oil. Stir-fry for 3 to 4 minutes. Turn into pasta bowl. Repeat with remaining olive oil and zucchini mixture.

Toss zucchini mixture with pasta. Sprinkle with pepper and Parmesan cheese. Serve immediately. Serves 4.

1 serving: 301 Calories; 7.5 g Total Fat; 262 mg Sodium; 11 g Protein; 48 g Carbohydrate; 4 g Dietary Fiber

VEGETABLE LASAGNE

This is a fabulous lasagne! It takes 1 to 1½ hours to prepare—but it's a real crowd-pleaser.

CREAM SAUCE

Can of skim evaporated milk	13½ oz.	385 mL
Skim milk	1½ cups	375 mL
All-purpose flour	¼ cup	60 mL
Grated light Parmesan cheese	3 tbsp.	50 mL
Onion powder	½ tsp.	2 mL
Salt	½ tsp.	2 mL
Garlic powder	¼ tsp.	1 mL

STEWED TOMATO SAUCE

Large onion, finely diced	1	1
Garlic cloves, minced	2	2
Olive oil	2 tsp.	10 mL
Large green pepper, finely diced	1	1
Medium red pepper, finely diced	1	1
Medium yellow pepper, finely diced	1	1
Dried whole oregano	1½ tsp.	7 mL
Dried sweet basil	1 tsp.	5 mL
Granulated sugar	1 tsp.	5 mL
Salt	½ tsp.	2 mL
Pepper	¼ tsp.	1 mL
Cans of stewed tomatoes (14 oz., 398 mL, each), with juice, chopped	3	3
Can of tomato sauce	7¼ oz.	213 mL
Medium zucchini, with peel	4	4
Boiling water	12 cups	3 L
Salt	1 tbsp.	15 mL
Lasagna noodles	12	12
Boiling water	20 cups	5 L
Salt	1½ tbsp.	25 mL
Grated part-skim mozzarella cheese	¾ cup	175 mL

Cream Sauce: Slowly whisk both milks into flour in medium saucepan until smooth. Heat and stir until boiling and thickened. Remove from heat. Stir in remaining 4 ingredients. Makes 3 cups (750 mL) sauce.

Stewed Tomato Sauce: Sauté onion and garlic in olive oil in large non-stick frying pan for 3 to 4 minutes until soft. Stir in peppers and next 5 ingredients. Cook for 2 minutes until peppers are tender-crisp. Add tomatoes and tomato sauce. Boil, uncovered, for 15 minutes until reduced and thickened. Makes 8 cups (2 L) sauce.

Cut zucchini, lengthwise, into ¼ inch (6 mm) slices. Blanch in first amounts of boiling water and salt in large uncovered pot or Dutch oven for 3 minutes. Drain. Rinse with cold water. Lay on tea towel or paper towel to dry well.

Cook lasagna noodles in second amounts of boiling water and salt in same pot for 10 minutes, stirring occasionally, until just tender.

Assemble in lightly greased 9 x 13 inch (22 x 33 cm) baking dish as follows:

1. ½ cup (125 mL) Stewed Tomato Sauce
2. 4 lasagna noodles
3. 2½ cups (625 mL) Stewed Tomato Sauce
4. 1 cup (250 mL) Cream Sauce
5. ½ of zucchini
6. 4 lasagna noodles
7. 2½ cups (625 mL) Stewed Tomato Sauce
8. 1 cup (250 mL) Cream Sauce
9. Remaining ½ of zucchini
10. 4 lasagna noodles
11. 2½ cups (625 mL) Stewed Tomato Sauce
12. 1 cup (250 mL) Cream Sauce
13. All of mozzarella cheese

Cover with lightly greased foil. Bake in 350°F (175°C) oven for 45 minutes. Remove foil. Bake for 10 to 15 minutes until cheese is melted and slightly golden. Let stand, uncovered, for 10 to 15 minutes before cutting. Serves 10.

1 serving: 248 Calories; 3.6 g Total Fat; 881 mg Sodium; 14 g Protein; 43 g Carbohydrate; 4 g Dietary Fiber

SEAFOOD LASAGNE

You will love the aroma while this casserole is baking! Rich sauce loaded with seafood.

Finely chopped onion	1½ cups	375 mL
Garlic clove, minced	1	1
Margarine (or butter)	2 tsp.	10 mL
Dry white (or alcohol-free) wine	½ cup	125 mL
All-purpose flour	⅓ cup	75 mL
Cornstarch	2 tbsp.	30 mL
Seafood bouillon powder	4 tsp.	20 mL
Parsley flakes	1 tbsp.	15 mL
Onion powder	½ tsp.	2 mL
Garlic powder	1/4 tsp.	1 mL
Can of skim evaporated milk	13½ oz.	385 mL
Skim milk	2½ cups	625 mL
Hot pepper sauce	¼ tsp.	1 mL
Small cooked shrimp, peeled and deveined	8 oz.	225 g
Cooked small scallops (see Note)	8 oz.	225 g
Cans of crabmeat, (4½ oz., 120 g, each), drained and cartilage removed, flaked	2	2
Spinach lasagna noodles	9	9
Boiling water	16 cups	4 L
Salt	4 tsp.	20 mL
Grated part-skim mozzarella cheese	⅓ cup	75 mL
Grated light Cheddar cheese	⅓ cup	75 mL

Sauté onion and garlic in margarine in medium frying pan for 3 minutes until onion is just starting to soften. Stir in wine. Cook, uncovered, for 10 minutes, stirring occasionally, until liquid is evaporated and onion is very soft.

Stir next 6 ingredients together in medium saucepan. Slowly whisk in both milks until smooth. Heat and stir until boiling and thickened. Stir in hot pepper sauce and onion mixture.

Spread ½ cup (125 mL) sauce in bottom of lightly greased 9 x 13 inch (22 x 33 cm) baking dish. In each of 3 small bowls, combine ⅓ (about 2 cups, 500 mL) of remaining sauce with shrimp, ⅓ (about 2 cups, 500 mL) with scallops and ⅓ (about 2 cups, 500 mL) with crabmeat.

Cook lasagna noodles in boiling water and salt in large uncovered pot or Dutch oven for 10 minutes, stirring occasionally, until just firm. Drain. Rinse with cold water. Drain.

Lay 3 noodles on sauce in baking dish. Cover with shrimp sauce. Repeat with layer of 3 noodles and layer of scallop sauce. Repeat with remaining 3 noodles and crab sauce. Top with both cheeses. Cover with lightly greased foil. Bake in 350°F (175°C) oven for 45 minutes. Remove foil. Bake, uncovered, for 10 to 15 minutes until cheese is browned. Let stand, uncovered, for 15 minutes before cutting. Serves 8.

1 serving: 285 Calories; 3.8 g Total Fat; 702 mg Sodium; 22 g Protein; 37 g Carbohydrate; 3 g Dietary Fiber

Note: To poach scallops, combine ⅓ cup (75 mL) water, ⅓ cup (75 mL) white (or alcohol-free) wine and 1 bay leaf in small saucepan. Simmer scallops for 1 to 2 minutes until just opaque. Drain. Discard bay leaf.

1. Rigatoni Broccoli Bake, page 79
2. Italian Steak, page 56
3. Stuffed Turkey Scallopini, page 65

Props Courtesy Of: Stokes
The Bay

CREAMY LASAGNE

This will become a favorite for those who don't like the cottage cheese layer in traditional lasagne.

TOMATO MEAT SAUCE

Lean ground beef	1 lb.	454 g
Chopped onion	1 cup	250 mL
Garlic cloves, minced	2	2
Chopped green pepper	1 cup	250 mL
Can of roma (plum) tomatoes, with juice, chopped	28 oz.	796 mL
Can of tomato paste	5½ oz.	156 mL
Dried sweet basil	2 tsp.	10 mL
Dried whole oregano	1 tsp.	5 mL
Granulated sugar	1 tsp.	5 mL
Salt	1 tsp.	5 mL
Pepper, sprinkle		

CREAM SAUCE

Can of skim evaporated milk	13½ oz.	385 mL
Skim milk	⅓ cup	75 mL
All-purpose flour	¼ cup	60 mL
Non-fat Italian dressing	3 tbsp.	50 mL
Grated light Parmesan cheese	2 tbsp.	30 mL
Lasagna noodles	9	9
Boiling water	16 cups	4 L
Salt	4 tsp.	20 mL
Grated part-skim mozzarella cheese	⅔ cup	150 mL

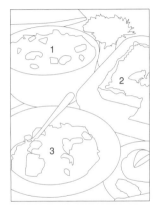

1. Italian Pasta Skillet, page 50
2. Spinach Lasagne, page 74
3. Chicken Fagioli Stew, page 67

Props Courtesy Of: The Bay

Tomato Meat Sauce: Scramble-fry ground beef, onion, garlic and green pepper in large non-stick frying pan for about 10 minutes until no pink remains in beef. Drain. Add next 7 ingredients. Reduce heat. Simmer, uncovered, for 20 minutes until slightly reduced. Makes about 6 cups (1.5 L) sauce.

Cream Sauce: Slowly whisk both milks into flour in medium saucepan until smooth. Heat and stir until boiling and thickened. Remove from heat. Stir in dressing and Parmesan cheese. Makes 2 cups (500 mL) sauce.

Cook lasagna noodles in boiling water and salt in large uncovered pot or Dutch oven for 10 minutes, stirring occasionally, just tender but firm. Drain. Rinse with cold water. Drain.

Assemble in lightly greased 9 x 13 inch (22 x 33 cm) baking dish in layers as follows:

1. 2 tbsp. (30 mL) Tomato Meat Sauce
2. 3 lasagna noodles
3. ⅓ of Tomato Meat Sauce
4. ⅓ of Cream Sauce
5. 3 lasagna noodles
6. ⅓ of Tomato Meat Sauce
7. ⅓ of Cream Sauce
8. 3 lasagna noodles
9. Remaining Tomato Meat Sauce
10. Remaining Cream Sauce
11. All of mozzarella cheese

Cover with lightly greased foil. Bake in 350°F (175°C) oven for 45 minutes. Remove foil. Broil for 4 to 5 minutes until cheese is browned slightly. Let stand, uncovered, for 15 minutes before cutting. Serves 10.

1 serving: *253 Calories; 6.1 g Total Fat; 597 mg Sodium; 19 g Protein; 32 g Carbohydrate; 3 g Dietary Fiber*

SPINACH LASAGNE

No meat in this. The green, red and white colors look so attractive. Good.

Lasagna noodles	10-12	10-12
Cooking oil (optional)	1 tbsp.	15 mL
Salt	1 tbsp.	15 mL
Boiling water	16 cups	4 L

TOMATO MUSHROOM SAUCE

Margarine (or butter)	2 tbsp.	30 mL
Chopped onion	1 cup	250 mL
Sliced fresh mushrooms	2 cups	500 mL
Cans of tomato sauce (7½ oz., 213 mL, each)	2	2
Can of tomato paste	5½ oz.	156 mL
Dried whole oregano	1 tsp.	5 mL
Salt	1 tsp.	5 mL
Granulated sugar	1 tsp.	5 mL
Dried sweet basil	¼ tsp.	1 mL

SPINACH LAYER

Dry curd cottage cheese	2 cups	500 mL
Large egg	1	1
Frozen chopped spinach, thawed and squeezed dry	10 oz.	300 g
Salt, sprinkle		
Pepper, sprinkle		
Ground nutmeg, light sprinkle		
Grated Parmesan cheese	½ cup	125 mL
Grated mozzarella cheese	2 cups	500 mL

Cook lasagna noodles, cooking oil and salt in boiling water in large uncovered pot or Dutch oven for 14 to 16 minutes until tender but firm. Drain.

Tomato Mushroom Sauce: Melt margarine in frying pan. Add onion. Sauté until onion is soft and clear.

Add mushrooms. Sauté for 3 to 5 minutes until soft.

Add next 6 ingredients. Stir. Reduce heat. Simmer, uncovered, for 10 to 15 minutes.

Spinach Layer: Combine cottage cheese and egg in medium bowl. Add spinach, salt, pepper and nutmeg. Mix.

To assemble, layer in greased 9 x 13 inch (22 x 33 cm) pan as follows:

1. ½ of noodles
2. ½ of Tomato Mushroom Sauce
3. All of Spinach Layer
4. ½ of noodles
5. ½ of Tomato Mushroom Sauce
6. All of Parmesan cheese
7. All of mozzarella cheese

Cover with greased foil. Bake in 350°F (175°C) oven for 50 to 60 minutes. Let stand for 10 minutes, uncovered, before cutting. Serves 12.

1 serving: 235 Calories; 9.6 g Total Fat; 829 mg Sodium; 16 g Protein; 22 g Carbohydrate; 2 g Dietary Fiber

Pictured on page 72.

Dry pasta can be stored in a tightly sealed container indefinitely.

Pasta With Lemon Vegetables

Great with any combination of vegetables.

Skim evaporated milk	1 cup	250 mL
Non-fat spreadable cream cheese	8 oz.	225 g
Cornstarch	2 tbsp.	30 mL
White (or alcohol-free) wine	2 tbsp.	30 mL
Low-fat chicken bouillon cube (⅓ oz., 10.5 g)	¼	¼
Boiling water	¼ cup	60 mL
Lemon juice	2 tbsp.	30 mL
Fresh broccoli florets	1 cup	250 mL
Sliced fresh asparagus, cut diagonally	1 cup	250 mL
Fresh pea pods	1 cup	250 mL
Sliced fresh green beans, cut diagonally	1 cup	250 mL
Grated lemon zest	1 tbsp.	15 mL
Rotini pasta, uncooked (about 8 oz., 225 g)	3 cups	750 mL
Freshly grated Parmesan cheese (optional)	2 tbsp.	30 mL
Pepper, sprinkle		

Heat evaporated milk in medium saucepan. Add cream cheese. Stir until melted. Stir cornstarch and wine together in small cup. Add to cream cheese mixture. Heat and stir until bubbling and thickened.

Dissolve bouillon in boiling water in small cup. Pour into non-stick frying pan or wok. Add lemon juice. Bring to a boil.

Add broccoli, asparagus, pea pods and green beans. Reduce heat. Cover. Simmer for 6 minutes, stirring once at half-time. Sprinkle lemon zest over top.

Cook pasta according to package directions. Drain.

Combine pasta, vegetables and sauce in large serving bowl. Sprinkle with Parmesan cheese and pepper. Serves 8.

1 serving: 207 Calories; 0.8 g Total Fat; 108 mg Sodium; 10 g Protein; 39 g Carbohydrate; 2 g Dietary Fiber

Chick Pea And Tomato Pasta

Only 15 minutes to prepare. To reduce sodium, omit the chick pea liquid and add ⅓ cup (75 mL) water.

Garlic cloves, minced	2	2
Small onion, slivered	1	1
Olive oil	1 tbsp.	15 mL
Can of diced tomatoes, with juice	28 oz.	796 mL
Finely chopped fresh parsley	¼ cup	60 mL
Dried sweet basil	1 tsp.	5 mL
Dried whole oregano	¾ tsp.	4 mL
Granulated sugar	½ tsp.	2 mL
Freshly ground pepper	¼ tsp.	1 mL
Can of chick peas (garbanzo beans), with liquid	19 oz.	540 mL
Rotini pasta, uncooked (about 10 oz., 285 g)	4 cups	1 L
Grated Parmesan cheese	2 tbsp.	30 mL

Sauté garlic and onion in olive oil in medium saucepan until onion is slightly soft. Stir in tomatoes with juice, parsley, basil, oregano, sugar and pepper. Bring to a boil. Reduce heat. Simmer, uncovered, for 15 minutes.

Add chick peas with liquid. Stir. Simmer for 10 minutes until thickened.

Cook pasta according to package directions. Drain. Combine pasta and sauce in large serving bowl. Sprinkle with Parmesan cheese. Serves 4.

1 serving: 542 Calories; 7.5 g Total Fat; 794 mg Sodium; 20 g Protein; 100 g Carbohydrate; 9 g Dietary Fiber

PERFECT PASTA PEPPERS

Very colorful. Use the same color of peppers or any combination of the four colors.

Orzo pasta	1 cup	250 mL
Boiling water	8 cups	2 L
Salt	2 tsp.	10 mL
Basil Pesto, page 91 (or commercial)	1 tbsp.	15 mL
Ripe medium roma (plum) tomatoes, diced	2	2
Chopped pitted ripe olives	2 tbsp.	30 mL
Chopped fresh parsley (or 1 tsp., 5 mL, flakes)	1 tbsp.	15 mL
Chopped fresh sweet basil (or 1 tsp., 5 mL, dried)	1 tbsp.	15 mL
Capers, rinsed and chopped (optional)	2 tsp.	10 mL
Salt	⅛ tsp.	0.5 mL
Freshly ground pepper, sprinkle		
Medium assorted peppers, similar in size and shape	3	3
Grated part-skim mozzarella cheese	½ cup	125 mL
Dry bread crumbs	2 tbsp.	30 mL

Cook pasta in boiling water and first amount of salt in large saucepan for 10 minutes, stirring occasionally, until tender but firm. Drain. Return to saucepan. Toss with pesto until coated. Stir in next 7 ingredients.

Cut peppers lengthwise through stem. Remove seeds and ribs from each half. Divide pasta mixture among 6 halves. Arrange in single layer in lightly greased shallow baking dish. Cover tightly with lid or seal with foil. Bake in 400°F (205°C) oven for 30 minutes until peppers are just tender-crisp.

Combine mozzarella cheese and bread crumbs in small bowl. Divide mixture among pepper halves. Return to oven. Bake until cheese is melted and bread crumbs are browned. Serves 6.

1 serving: 224 Calories; 4 g Total Fat; 59 mg Sodium; 9 g Protein; 38 g Carbohydrate; 2 g Dietary Fiber

PASTA MARGARITA

This dish is the color of the Italian flag—red, green and white.

Linguine pasta	8 oz.	225 g
Boiling water	8 cups	2 L
Salt	2 tsp.	10 mL
Water	¼ cup	60 mL
Vegetable bouillon powder	½ tsp.	2 mL
Garlic cloves, minced	2	2
Cornstarch	2 tsp.	10 mL
Water	¼ cup	60 mL
Fresh spinach leaves, stems removed, lightly packed	8 cups	2 L
Diced ripe roma (plum) tomato	3 cups	750 mL
Dried whole oregano	¼ - ½ tsp.	1-2 mL
Salt, sprinkle		
Freshly ground pepper, sprinkle		
Pine nuts, toasted and chopped (optional)	2 tbsp.	30 mL

Cook linguine in boiling water and first amount of salt in large uncovered pot or Dutch oven for 8 to 10 minutes, stirring occasionally, until tender but firm. Drain. Keep warm.

Heat first amount of water and bouillon powder in large non-stick frying pan. Sauté garlic for about 2 minutes until soft.

Combine cornstarch and second amount of water in small bowl. Add to garlic mixture. Heat and stir until boiling and thickened.

Stir in spinach. Cover. Cook for 2 to 3 minutes until spinach is just limp. Do not overcook. Add tomato and oregano. Stir gently. Cover. Cook for 3 minutes until tomato is warm.

Sprinkle with second amount of salt and pepper. Spoon over pasta. Toss. Sprinkle with pine nuts. Serves 4.

1 serving: 255 Calories; 1.5 g Total Fat; 144 mg Sodium; 10 g Protein; 51 g Carbohydrate; 5 g Dietary Fiber

SPINACH AND CHEESE CAPPELLETTI

Cute little hats stuffed with a green and white filling.

FILLING

Garlic clove, minced (optional)	1	1
Finely chopped onion	2 tbsp.	30 mL
Margarine (or butter)	1 tsp.	5 mL
Package of frozen spinach, (10 oz., 300 g), thawed, squeezed dry and finely chopped	⅓	⅓
Dry curd cottage cheese	½ cup	125 mL
Egg white (large)	1	1
Non-fat spreadable cream cheese	2 tbsp.	30 mL
Grated light Parmesan cheese	1 tbsp.	15 mL
Salt	¾ tsp.	4 mL
Parsley flakes	¼ tsp.	1 mL
Dried marjoram, crushed	¼ tsp.	1 mL
Dried sweet basil, crushed	¼ tsp.	1 mL
Freshly ground pepper, sprinkle		
Prepared Egg Pasta Dough, page 96 (or Basic Pasta Dough, page 97), about ⅓ of recipe	½ lb.	225 g
Boiling water	12 cups	3 L
Salt	1 tbsp.	15 mL

Filling: Sauté garlic and onion in margarine in non-stick frying pan until onion is soft. Stir in spinach. Cook for 30 seconds to dry.

Put next 9 ingredients into blender. Add spinach mixture. Process, with an on/off motion, until spinach is well chopped and cheeses are evenly moistened. Makes ¾ cup (175 mL) filling.

1. Roll out ¼ of rested dough into very thin 12 x 16 inch (30 x 40 cm) rectangle. Cut 2 inch (5 cm) wide strips. Place slightly rounded ¼ tsp. (1 mL) filling, about 1½ inches (3.8 cm) apart, on dough starting ¾ inch (2 cm) from one edge. Cut dough between dabs of filling with sharp knife to form squares.

2. Moisten 2 adjacent sides of each square with water. Fold moistened edge diagonally over filling.

3a). Seal edges, making small filled triangle.

3b). Bend each triangle around finger, at fold, and pinch 2 ends together, making sure pointy corner is up to resemble tiny hat. Repeat until all dough and filling are used. Keep in single layer on floured tray, covered with tea towel, until ready to cook.

Cook cappelletti, in 2 batches, in gently boiling water and second amount of salt in large uncovered pot or Dutch oven for 2 to 3 minutes, stirring occasionally, until tender but firm. Remove with slotted spoon to colander. Rinse with hot water. Drain. Makes about 130 cappaletti. Serves 8.

1 serving: 90 Calories; 0.9 g Total Fat; 424 mg Sodium; 6 g Protein; 14 g Carbohydrate; 1 g Dietary Fiber

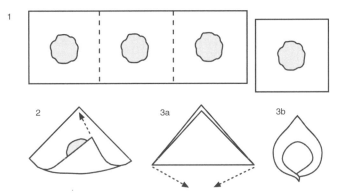

JUMBO CHEESE SHELLS

You can find jumbo shell pasta at Italian specialty stores.

Skim evaporated milk	¾ cup	175 mL
All-purpose flour	4 tsp.	20 mL
Finely chopped onion	½ cup	125 mL
Garlic clove, minced	1	1
Olive oil	1 tsp.	5 mL
Can of roma (plum) tomatoes, with juice, processed	14 oz.	398 mL
Finely chopped fresh sweet basil (or 1 tbsp., 15 mL, dried)	¼ cup	60 mL
Salt	¼ tsp.	1 mL
Jumbo shell pasta (about 8 oz., 225 g)	24	24
Boiling water	12 cups	3 L
Salt	1 tbsp.	15 mL
Part-skim ricotta cheese	1 cup	250 mL
Non-fat creamed cottage cheese, sieved or mashed	1 cup	250 mL
Egg whites (large), fork-beaten	2	2
Grated light Parmesan cheese	1 tbsp.	15 mL
Salt, sprinkle		
Pepper	¹⁄₁₆ tsp.	0.5 mL

Chopped chives, for garnish

Slowly whisk evaporated milk into flour in small saucepan on medium until boiling and thickened. Remove from heat. Cover.

Sauté onion and garlic in olive oil in medium non-stick frying pan until onion is soft. Stir in tomatoes, basil and first amount of salt. Reduce heat. Cover. Simmer for 10 minutes. Stir in milk mixture. Heat, stirring constantly, until boiling and thickened. Pour into ungreased 9 x 13 inch (22 x 33 cm) baking dish. Makes 2 cups (500 mL) sauce.

Cook pasta in boiling water and second amount of salt in large saucepan for 10 to 12 minutes, stirring carefully to prevent shells from ripping, until tender but firm. Do not overcook. Drain. Rinse with cold water. Turn upside down on clean dry cloth to drain well.

Combine remaining 6 ingredients in small bowl. Mix well. Fill each shell with rounded tablespoonful of cheese mixture. Arrange shells on tomato sauce in baking dish. Cover with foil. Bake in 350°F (175°C) oven for 50 minutes. Sprinkle individual servings with chives. Serves 4 to 6.

1 serving: 457 Calories; 7.9 g Total Fat; 645 mg Sodium; 34 g Protein; 63 g Carbohydrate; 3 g Dietary Fiber

Pictured on page 54.

Salt helps prevent nutrients from leaching out of the pasta into the cooking water.

RIGATONI BROCCOLI BAKE

A nice and creamy dish. Green shows throughout.
Good choice.

Rigatoni pasta (about 8 oz., 225 g)	3½ cups	875 mL
Cooking oil (optional)	1 tbsp.	15 mL
Salt	2 tsp.	10 mL
Boiling water	10 cups	2.5 L
Margarine (or butter)	⅓ cup	75 mL
All-purpose flour	⅓ cup	75 mL
Milk	3 cups	750 mL
Grated Parmesan cheese	¾ cup	175 mL
Salt	1 tsp.	5 mL
Garlic salt	½ tsp.	2 mL
Ground nutmeg	⅛ tsp.	0.5 mL
Dried thyme	⅛ tsp.	0.5 mL
Grated sharp Cheddar cheese	1½ cups	375 mL
Fresh broccoli, cut up (or two 10 oz., 300 g, each, frozen packages), cooked	1½ lbs.	680 g
Grated Swiss cheese	¾ cup	175 mL

Cook pasta, cooking oil and first amount of salt in boiling water in large uncovered pot or Dutch oven for 12 to 15 minutes, stirring occasionally, until tender but firm. Drain. Return to pot.

Melt margarine in medium saucepan. Mix in flour. Stir in milk until boiling and thickened.

Add Parmesan cheese, second amount of salt, garlic salt, nutmeg, thyme and Cheddar cheese. Stir. Add to pasta. Stir.

Add broccoli. Mix well. Pour into greased 9 x 13 inch (22 x 33 cm) pan.

Sprinkle with Swiss cheese. Bake, uncovered, in 350°F (175°C) oven for about 20 minutes until cheese is melted. Cuts into 15 pieces.

1 piece: 218 Calories; 10.9 g Total Fat; 489 mg Sodium; 11 g Protein; 20 g Carbohydrate; 2 g Dietary Fiber

Pictured on page 71.

BAKED MOZZA RIGATONI

A great creamy cheese sauce you would never believe was low in fat! Very quick and easy.

Skim milk	½ cup	125 mL
All-purpose flour	3 tbsp.	50 mL
Skim milk	1 cup	250 mL
Salt	½ tsp.	2 mL
Onion powder	¼ tsp.	1 mL
Grated part-skim mozzarella cheese	1 cup	250 mL
Rigatoni pasta (about 10 oz., 285 g)	4 cups	1 L
Boiling water	10 cups	2.5 L
Salt	2½ tsp.	12 mL
Paprika, sprinkle (optional)		

Combine first amount of milk and flour in small saucepan. Mix well until smooth. Add second amount of milk, first amount of salt and onion powder. Heat and stir until boiling and slightly thickened.

Add cheese. Stir until melted.

Cook pasta in boiling water and second amount of salt in large uncovered pot or Dutch oven for 9 to 11 minutes, stirring occasionally, until tender but firm. Drain. Turn into lightly greased 2 quart (2 L) shallow casserole dish. Pour sauce over top. Sprinkle with paprika. Cover. Bake in 375°F (190°C) oven for 15 minutes. Remove cover. Bake for 10 minutes until cheese is bubbling. Serves 4.

1 serving: 399 Calories; 6.3 g Total Fat; 539 mg Sodium; 21 g Protein; 63 g Carbohydrate; 2 g Dietary Fiber

SPINACH-STUFFED CANNELLONI

Assemble everything the day before or morning of. Cover and chill. Bake when needed. To fill cannelloni shells, try using a plastic freezer bag with 1 corner cut off, or pastry bag with a large tip.

TOMATO SAUCE

Can of stewed tomatoes, mashed or processed	28 oz.	796 mL
Water	1 cup	250 mL
Brown sugar, packed	1 tsp.	5 mL
Whole cloves	2	2
Garlic clove, minced	1	1
Dried whole oregano	½ tsp.	2 mL

SPINACH FILLING

Finely chopped onion	⅓ cup	75 mL
Olive oil	1 tsp.	5 mL
Frozen chopped spinach, thawed and squeezed dry	10 oz.	300 g
Non-fat spreadable cream cheese	½ cup	125 mL
Non-fat creamed cottage cheese, mashed	1 cup	250 mL
Egg whites (large), fork-beaten	2	2
Grated light Parmesan cheese	1 tbsp.	15 mL
Salt	½ tsp.	2 mL
Pepper	⅛ tsp.	0.5 mL
Ground nutmeg	⅛ tsp.	0.5 mL
Oven-ready cannelloni shells	15	15
Grated part-skim mozzarella cheese	½ cup	125 mL

Tomato Sauce: Combine all 6 ingredients in medium saucepan. Cover. Simmer for 30 minutes. Discard cloves. Pour ½ of sauce into ungreased 2 quart (2 L) shallow casserole dish or 9 x 13 inch (22 x 33 cm) baking dish. Reserve remaining ½ of sauce.

Spinach Filling: Sauté onion in olive oil in large non-stick frying pan until soft. Add spinach. Heat and stir until liquid is evaporated. Remove from heat. Add cream cheese. Stir until cheese is melted.

Add cottage cheese, egg whites, Parmesan cheese, salt, pepper and nutmeg. Stir.

Divide and spoon filling into each cannelloni. Arrange in single layer on tomato sauce in casserole dish. Drizzle with remaining sauce, making sure there is some on every cannelloni. Cover with lightly greased foil. Bake in 350°F (175°C) oven for 40 minutes until pasta is tender and liquid is almost evaporated. Remove foil. Sprinkle with mozzarella cheese. Bake, uncovered, for 5 to 10 minutes until cheese is melted. Makes 15 cannelloni.

1 cannelloni with sauce: 93 Calories; 1.4 g Total Fat; 257 mg Sodium; 7 g Protein; 13 g Carbohydrate; 2 g Dietary Fiber

Most cooked (or frozen, thawed) spinach needs to be squeezed dry before adding to recipes. To do this, squeeze a small amount of spinach in one hand several times until most of the moisture is gone.

SPINACH PASTA ROLL

Looks so special. This makes two rolls. May be halved easily. Slice and serve with your favorite sauce.

Prepared Egg Pasta Dough, page 96

Packages of frozen chopped spinach (10 oz., 300 g, each), cooked and squeezed dry	2	2
Ricotta (or creamed cottage) cheese	1 cup	250 mL
Grated Parmesan cheese	¼ cup	60 mL
Salt	1 tsp.	5 mL
Pepper	¼ tsp.	1 mL
Ground nutmeg	¼ tsp.	1 mL

Boiling water, to cover		
Salt	2 tsp.	10 mL

Bolognese Sauce, page 86

Roll rested dough quite thin into rectangle 9 x 12 inches (22 x 30 cm).

Mix next 6 ingredients in medium bowl. Spread ½ on pasta to within 1 inch (2.5 cm) from edges. Roll up from short end, like jelly roll. Press ends and lengthwise edge to seal. Wrap in cheesecloth or disposable dishcloth. Tie ends with string. Repeat for second roll.

Add to boiling water and second amount of salt in uncovered fish poacher or roaster. Cook for about 30 minutes. Add more boiling water partway through cooking, if needed, to keep rolls covered. Drain. Let stand for 10 minutes before slicing. Arrange in greased 9 x 13 inch (22 x 33 cm) baking dish.

Pour Bolognese Sauce over slices. Cover with foil. Bake in 350°F (175°C) oven for about 30 minutes until hot. Serves 4.

1 serving with sauce: 739 Calories; 28.1 g Total Fat; 1705 mg Sodium; 36 g Protein; 30 g Carbohydrate; 5 g Dietary Fiber

Pictured on page 54.

TOMATO ZUCCHINI PASTA

Lots of eye appeal to this appetizing dish.

Spaccatella (or medium egg noodles)	8 oz.	225 g
Cooking oil (optional)	1 tbsp.	15 mL
Salt	2 tsp.	10 mL
Boiling water	10 cups	2.5 L
Chopped onion	1 cup	250 mL
Green pepper, chopped	1	1
Margarine (or butter)	½ cup	125 mL
Sliced zucchini, with peel	5 cups	1.25 L
Cherry tomatoes, halved	12	12
Grated Gruyère (or Swiss) cheese	1 cup	250 mL
Grated Parmesan cheese	¾ cup	175 mL
Chopped fresh parsley	½ cup	125 mL
Salt	1 tsp.	5 mL

Grated Parmesan cheese, sprinkle

Cook spaccatella, cooking oil and first amount of salt in boiling water in uncovered large pot or Dutch oven for 5 to 7 minutes, stirring occasionally, until tender but firm. Drain. Return to pot.

Sauté onion and green pepper in margarine in separate large uncovered pot or Dutch oven until onion is clear.

Add zucchini, tomato, Gruyère cheese, first amount of Parmesan cheese, parsley and second amount of salt. Sauté until cheese is melted. Add to pasta. Stir.

Put into 3 quart (3 L) greased casserole. Sprinkle with remaining Parmesan cheese. Cover. Bake in 350°F (175°C) oven for 30 to 40 minutes. Serves 6.

1 serving: 481 Calories; 28.5 g Total Fat; 972 mg Sodium; 19 g Protein; 39 g Carbohydrate; 4 g Dietary Fiber

Pasta Primavera

A grand dish. Great any time of year.

Coarsely chopped broccoli (or fresh asparagus)	2 cups	500 mL
Zucchini (about 1 medium), with peel, cut into fingers	2 cups	500 mL
Frozen (or fresh) pea pods	6 oz.	170 g
Frozen (or fresh) peas	1 cup	250 mL
Salt	1 tsp.	5 mL
Boiling water		
Cherry tomatoes, halved	12	12
Chopped fresh parsley	¼ cup	60 mL
Garlic clove, minced (or ¼ tsp., 1 mL, garlic powder)	1	1
Olive oil	1 tbsp.	15 mL
Olive oil	2 tbsp.	30 mL
Garlic clove, minced (or ¼ tsp., 1 mL, garlic powder)	1	1
Sliced fresh mushrooms	2 cups	500 mL
Spaghetti (or linguini) pasta	1 lb.	454 g
Cooking oil (optional)	1 tbsp.	15 mL
Salt	1 tbsp.	15 mL
Boiling water	16 cups	4 L
Whipping cream	1 cup	250 mL
Grated Parmesan cheese	½ cup	125 mL
Salt, generous sprinkle		
Pepper, sprinkle		
Dried sweet basil	2 tsp.	10 mL
Freshly grated Parmesan cheese, sprinkle		

Cook broccoli, zucchini, pea pods, peas and first amount of salt in 2 inches (5 cm) boiling water in large uncovered pot or Dutch oven for 3 minutes until tender-crisp. Drain. Set aside.

Sauté tomato, parsley and first garlic clove in first amount of olive oil in medium saucepan for about 5 minutes.

Heat second amount of olive oil in frying pan or wok. Sauté second garlic clove and mushrooms until soft. Add broccoli, zucchini, pea pods, peas and tomato mixture. Heat, stirring often, until heated through.

Cook spaghetti, cooking oil and second amount of salt in boiling water in large uncovered pot or Dutch oven for 11 to 13 minutes, stirring occasionally, until tender but firm. Drain.

Combine spaghetti with mushroom mixture. Add cream, first amount of Parmesan cheese, third amount of salt, pepper and basil. Toss gently to coat. Turn into serving bowl.

Sprinkle with Parmesan cheese. Serves 4.

1 serving: 899 Calories; 37.3 g Total Fat; 344 mg Sodium; 30 g Protein; 113 g Carbohydrate; 10 g Dietary Fiber

Pictured on page 53.

Look for seasonally shaped pasta to make a dish special. There are pumpkin shapes for Halloween and hearts for Valentine's Day. Substitute them for any similar sized pasta in a recipe.

★★

PASTA PRIMAVERA

A huge, colorful mixture of pasta and vegetables.
Makes a great meal. Low-fat version.

Chopped fresh broccoli	6 cups	1.5 L
Slivered zucchini, with peel	3 cups	750 mL
Frozen peas	2 cups	500 mL
Salt	1 tsp.	5 mL
Boiling water		
Cooking oil	1 tbsp.	15 mL
Garlic clove, minced	1	1
Sliced fresh mushrooms	2 cups	500 mL
Can of diced tomatoes, drained	14 oz.	398 mL
Chopped fresh parsley	¼ cup	60 mL
Linguine pasta	1 lb.	454 g
Boiling water	16 cups	4 L
Cooking oil (optional)	1 tbsp.	15 mL
Salt	1 tbsp.	15 mL
Can of skim evaporated milk	13½ oz.	385 mL
Grated Parmesan cheese	½ cup	125 mL
Salt	1 tsp.	5 mL

Grated Parmesan cheese, sprinkle

Cook broccoli, zucchini, peas and first amount of salt in 2 inches (5 cm) boiling water in medium saucepan for 3 minutes until tender-crisp. Drain. Set aside.

Heat cooking oil in wok or frying pan. Add garlic and mushrooms. Sauté until soft and moisture has evaporated.

Add tomatoes and parsley. Sauté for 1 minute. Remove from heat.

Cook linguini in boiling water, cooking oil and second amount of salt in large uncovered pot or Dutch oven for 9 to 11 minutes, stirring occasionally, until tender but firm. Drain. Add to wok. Add vegetables.

Add evaporated milk, first amount of Parmesan cheese and third amount of salt to wok. Heat and stir until mixture simmers. Simmer for about 3 minutes until slightly thickened. Turn into large bowl.

Sprinkle with second amount of Parmesan cheese. Makes 13 cups (3.25 L).

1 cup (250 mL): 228 Calories; 3.5 g Total Fat; 518 mg Sodium; 12 g Protein; 38 g Carbohydrate; 4 g Fiber

EASY PASTA PRIMAVERA

Frozen vegetables make this a very easy and quick dish to prepare.

Frozen Italian-style vegetables	2¼ lbs.	1 kg
Water	¼ cup	60 mL
Diet tub margarine	2 tbsp.	30 mL
Dried sweet basil	¼ tsp.	1 mL
Dried whole oregano	¼ tsp.	1 mL
Frozen egg product, thawed	6 tbsp.	100 mL
Skim evaporated milk	½ cup	125 mL
Grated light Parmesan cheese	¼ cup	60 mL
Spaghetti	10 oz.	285 g
Boiling water	12 cups	3 L
Salt	1 tbsp.	15 mL
Ripe small roma (plum) tomatoes, diced	2-3	2-3
Finely chopped fresh parsley	1 tbsp.	15 mL

Place vegetables and water in 2 quart (2 L) microwave-safe casserole dish. Cover. Microwave on high (100%) for 6 minutes. Drain.

Melt margarine in large non-stick frying pan. Add vegetables. Sprinkle with basil and oregano. Cook for about 5 minutes, stirring often, until tender.

Beat egg product, evaporated milk and Parmesan cheese together in small bowl.

Cook pasta in boiling water and salt in large uncovered pot or Dutch oven for 8 to 10 minutes, stirring occasionally, until tender but firm. Drain. Return to pot. Add milk mixture. Stir well.

Add vegetables, tomato and parsley. Toss until liquid is absorbed. Serves 4.

1 serving: 509 Calories; 5.7 g Total Fat; 367 mg Sodium; 25 g Protein; 93 g Carbohydrate; 12 g Dietary Fiber

LEEK AND SPINACH MANICOTTI

Bright green filling. Lots of sauce. To fill manicotti shells, try using a plastic freezer bag with 1 corner cut off, or pastry bag with a large tip.

Finely sliced leek (white and tender green parts only), see Tip, page 84	3 cups	750 mL
Garlic cloves, minced	2	2
Olive oil	2 tsp.	10 mL
Water	1 tbsp.	15 mL
Fresh spinach leaves, well packed, coarsely chopped	6 cups	1.5 L
Non-fat herb-flavored spreadable cream cheese	¼ cup	60 mL
Dry curd cottage cheese	1½ cups	375 mL
Egg whites (large)	2	2
Salt	½ tsp.	2 mL
Dried sweet basil	½ tsp.	2 mL
Dried whole oregano	¼ tsp.	1 mL
Ground nutmeg, pinch		
Manicotti pasta shells	14	14
Boiling water	12 cups	3 L
Salt	1 tbsp.	15 mL
Finely chopped onion	¼ cup	60 mL
Olive oil	1 tsp.	5 mL
Can of tomatoes, with juice, processed	28 oz.	796 mL
Salt	½ tsp.	2 mL
Granulated sugar, pinch		
Grated part-skim mozzarella cheese	½ cup	125 mL

Sauté leek and garlic in first amount of olive oil and water in large non-stick frying pan for about 15 minutes until leek is tender. Stir in spinach. Cover. Cook for 5 minutes until spinach is wilted. Remove cover. Cook for about 1 minute until liquid is evaporated. Stir in cream cheese until melted.

Mix cottage cheese and egg whites in small bowl until quite smooth. Stir into spinach mixture. Add first amount of salt, basil, oregano and nutmeg. Stir well.

Cook manicotti, in 2 batches, in boiling water and second amount of salt in large uncovered pot or Dutch oven for 7 minutes, stirring occasionally. Pasta should still be quite firm. Drain. Rinse in cold water. Drain well. Spoon ¼ cup (60 mL) filling into each manicotti. Place in single layer in lightly greased 9 x 13 inch (22 x 33 cm) baking dish.

Sauté onion in second amount of olive oil in large non-stick frying pan until soft. Add tomatoes, third amount of salt and sugar. Boil rapidly, uncovered, for 1 minute. Pour over manicotti. Sprinkle with cheese. Cover tightly with lightly greased foil. Bake in 350°F (175°C) oven for 30 minutes until hot and bubbling. Makes 14 manicotti.

1 manicotti with sauce: *132 Calories; 2.3 g Total Fat; 340 mg Sodium; 8 g Protein; 20 g Carbohydrate; 2 g Dietary Fiber*

Clean leeks by first removing wilted outer leaves. Trim off green tops and rootlets. Make several slices lengthwise, stopping about ¾ inch (2 cm) from the base. Rinse under cold water, separating layers to remove any dirt. Drain.

Pasta Sauces

ike paint to an artist's blank canvas, these Italian sauces will decorate pasta of all shapes. Spicy Spaghetti Sauce, page 86, has the chunky texture and herbs just begging for a plate of pasta and a slice of garlic bread. Or look to Scampi Sauce, page 87, for a blend of garlic, lemon and wine.

SUN-DRIED TOMATO SAUCE

A nice spicy sauce.

Garlic clove, minced	1	1
Crushed dried chilies	⅛-¼ tsp.	0.5-1 mL
Green onions, sliced	2	2
Sun-dried tomato halves, chopped (see Note)	4	4
Olive oil	2 tsp.	10 mL
Rosé (or white) wine	⅓ cup	75 mL
Juice of 1 medium orange		
Grated orange peel	2 tsp.	10 mL
Water	⅓ cup	75 mL
Chicken bouillon powder	½ tsp.	2 mL
Tomato paste	1 tbsp.	15 mL
Seeded and diced tomato	2 cups	500 mL
Freshly ground pepper, sprinkle		

Sauté garlic, chilies, green onion and sun-dried tomato in olive oil in large non-stick frying pan for 3 minutes.

Add next 6 ingredients. Bring to a boil. Reduce heat. Simmer, uncovered, for 2 minutes.

Add tomato and pepper. Stir until warm. Makes 2½ cups (625 mL).

½ cup (125 mL): 72 Calories; 2.8 g Total Fat; 95 mg Sodium; 1 g Protein; 8 g Carbohydrate; 2 g Dietary Fiber

Note: If the sun-dried tomatoes are too hard to chop, use kitchen scissors to cut into small pieces.

BOLOGNESE SAUCE

This ragu sauce is a good version of the real thing.

Bacon slices, diced	2	2
Finely chopped onion	1 cup	250 mL
Finely chopped celery	½ cup	125 mL
Grated carrot	½ cup	125 mL
Lean ground beef	1½ lbs.	680 g
Milk	1 cup	250 mL
Margarine (or butter)	2 tbsp.	30 mL
Salt	1 tsp.	5 mL
Pepper	¼ tsp.	1 mL
Ground nutmeg	⅛ tsp.	0.5 mL
Can of diced tomatoes, with juice	14 oz.	398 mL
Dry white (or alcohol-free) wine	2 tbsp.	30 mL

Sauté bacon, onion, celery and carrot in non-stick frying pan until onion is soft.

Add ground beef. Scramble-fry until no pink remains in beef.

Add milk, margarine, salt, pepper and nutmeg. Reduce heat. Simmer for about 30 minutes, stirring often, until most of moisture has evaporated.

Add tomatoes and wine. Cover. Simmer gently for about 30 minutes, stirring occasionally. Makes 4 cups (1 L).

1 cup (250 mL): 516 Calories; 34.1 g Total Fat; 1127 mg Sodium; 37 g Protein; 13 g Carbohydrate; 2 g Dietary Fiber

SPICY SPAGHETTI SAUCE

Serve this over spaghetti, noodles or other pasta. A chunky sauce.

Can of diced tomatoes, with juice	19 oz.	540 mL
Ketchup	¼ cup	60 mL
Can of sliced mushrooms, drained	10 oz.	284 mL
Chopped green pepper	⅓ cup	75 mL
Lemon juice	1½ tbsp.	25 mL
Dried whole oregano	¾ tsp.	4 mL
Dried sweet basil	½ tsp.	2 mL
Bay leaf	1	1
Chili powder	2 tsp.	10 mL
Garlic powder	¼ tsp.	1 mL
Granulated sugar (optional)	1 tsp.	5 mL
Salt	1½ tsp.	7 mL
Pepper	¼ tsp.	1 mL
Lean ground beef	1 lb.	454 g
Chopped onion	1 cup	250 mL

Combine first 13 ingredients in 3½ quart (3.5 L) slow cooker.

Scramble-fry ground beef and onion in non-stick frying pan until no pink remains in beef. Drain well. Add to slow cooker. Stir. Cover. Cook on Low for 6 to 7 hours or on High for 3 to 3½ hours. Discard bay leaf. Makes 5¼ cups (1.3 L).

1 cup (250 mL): 193 Calories; 7.8 g Total Fat; 1267 mg Sodium; 18 g Protein; 14 g Carbohydrate; 3 g Dietary Fiber

To bring down the heat in your mouth caused by chili peppers, drink or eat dairy products. Water only spreads the hot oil compound known as capsaicin and provides no relief.

Italian

SCAMPI SAUCE

Refreshing garlic, lemon and wine-flavored sauce. Perfect with angel hair pasta.

Garlic cloves, finely chopped	3	3
Olive oil	1 tsp.	5 mL
Water	1 cup	250 mL
Seafood bouillon powder	1 tbsp.	15 mL
Granulated sugar	1½ tbsp.	25 mL
Dry white (or alcohol-free) wine	½ cup	125 mL
Cornstarch	2 tbsp.	30 mL
Grated lemon peel	4 tsp.	20 mL
Finely sliced fresh chives	2 tbsp.	30 mL
Cooked prawns, shelled and deveined	12 oz.	340 g

Sauté garlic in olive oil in medium non-stick frying pan until soft. Add water, bouillon powder and sugar. Heat, uncovered, until simmering.

Combine wine and cornstarch in small cup. Stir into garlic mixture. Heat and stir until boiling and slightly thickened. Remove from heat.

Stir in lemon peel, chives and prawns. Heat for 1 minute. Makes 2½ cups (625 mL).

½ cup (125 mL): 162 Calories; 2.3 g Total Fat; 639 mg Sodium; 18 g Protein; 11 g Carbohydrate; trace g Dietary Fiber

BEEF AND MUSHROOM SAUCE

Very appealing. Wonderful mushroom taste.

Lean tender beef (top sirloin or tenderloin), thinly sliced into strips	10 oz.	285 g
Finely chopped onion	¼ cup	60 mL
Garlic cloves, minced	2	2
Cooking oil	1 tsp.	5 mL
Large fresh portobello mushrooms	2	2
Pepper, sprinkle		
Beef bouillon powder	2 tsp.	10 mL
Skim milk	1 cup	250 mL
All-purpose flour	2 tbsp.	30 mL
Skim evaporated milk	½ cup	125 mL

Sauté beef strips, onion and garlic in cooking oil in large non-stick frying pan for about 3 minutes until onion is soft.

Prepare mushrooms by trimming stem and dark "gills" off with sharp knife. Rinse. Blot dry. Dice mushrooms into about ½ inch (12 mm) pieces. Add to beef. Sprinkle with pepper. Simmer, stirring frequently, for 2 to 3 minutes until liquid is released from mushrooms. Stir in bouillon powder. Simmer until almost all liquid is evaporated.

Whisk milk into flour in small bowl until smooth. Pour into mushroom mixture along with evaporated milk. Cook, stirring frequently, until boiling and thickened. Makes 4 cups (1 L).

1 cup (250 mL): 193 Calories; 4.6 g Total Fat; 418 mg Sodium; 22 g Protein; 15 g Carbohydrate; 1 g Dietary Fiber

SHRIMP SAUCE

This red Creole-style sauce is exceptional.

Green pepper, chopped	1	1
Chopped onion	½ cup	125 mL
Margarine (or butter)	¼ cup	60 mL
Can of diced tomatoes, with juice	14 oz.	398 mL
Salt	1 tsp.	5 mL
Pepper	¼ tsp.	1 mL
Dried whole oregano	½ tsp.	2 mL
Dried sweet basil	½ tsp.	2 mL
Garlic powder	1½ tsp.	7 mL
Cocktail size shrimp, fresh or frozen, thawed	½ lb.	225 g
Can of tomato sauce	7½ oz.	213 mL
Parsley flakes	2 tsp.	10 mL

Sauté green pepper and onion in margarine in medium saucepan until soft.

Add next 6 ingredients. Simmer, uncovered, for 20 to 30 minutes until liquid is almost gone.

Add shrimp, tomato sauce and parsley. Simmer for 15 minutes. Makes 3 cups (750 mL).

1 cup (250 mL): 221 Calories; 17 g Total Fat; 1766 mg Sodium; 4 g Protein; 17 g Carbohydrate; 3 g Dietary Fiber

Pictured on page 89.

ALFREDO SAUCE

Delicately flavored, delicate looking. A grand sauce for over fettuccine.

Margarine (or butter)	½ cup	125 mL
Whipping cream	1 cup	250 mL
Grated Parmesan cheese	½ cup	125 mL
Salt	½ -1 tsp.	2-5 mL
Pepper	¼ tsp.	1 mL
Chopped fresh parsley	2 tbsp.	30 mL

Combine margarine and whipping cream in small saucepan. Bring to a gentle simmer on medium-low.

Add remaining 4 ingredients. Stir to heat through. Makes 2¼ cups (550 mL).

1 cup (250 mL): 313 Calories; 32.4 g Total Fat; 597 mg Sodium; 5 g Protein; 2 g Carbohydrate; trace Dietary Fiber

1. Shrimp Sauce, this page
2. Yellow Pepper Sauce, page 94
3. Tomato Meatball Sauce, page 93
4. Basil Pesto, page 91

CHEESE SAUCE WITH BACON

Serve this creamy sauce over Gnocchi, page 103.

Margarine (or butter)	3 tbsp.	50 mL
All-purpose flour	3 tbsp.	50 mL
Salt	½ tsp.	2 mL
Pepper	⅛ tsp.	0.5 mL
Milk	2 cups	500 mL
Grated medium Cheddar cheese	1 cup	250 mL
Bacon slices, cooked crisp and crumbled	4-6	4-6

Melt margarine in medium saucepan. Mix in flour, salt and pepper until smooth. Stir in milk until boiling and thickened. Stir in cheese until melted.

Add bacon. Stir. Makes 3 cups (750 mL).

½ cup (125 mL): 207 Calories; 15.5 g Total Fat; 529 mg Sodium; 10 g Protein; 8 g Carbohydrate; trace Dietary Fiber

CREAMY CHEESE SAUCE

Fabulous flavor. Creamy rich with a taste of bacon. Excellent over fettuccine.

Whipping cream	1 cup	250 mL
Process cheese loaf, cut up	8 oz.	225 g
Bacon slices, cooked crisp and crumbled	8	8

Heat cream, cheese loaf and bacon in medium saucepan until cheese is melted. Makes about 2 cups (500 mL).

½ cup (125 mL): 117 Calories; 10.5 g Total Fat; 306 mg Sodium; 4 g Protein; 2 g Carbohydrate; 0 g Dietary Fiber

BASIL PESTO

Great with linguine. Make double the amount and freeze in small quantities to flavor other sauces.

Olive oil	2 tbsp.	30 mL
Garlic clove, halved	1	1
Fresh sweet basil, firmly packed	½ cup	125 mL
Grated light Parmesan cheese	2 tbsp.	30 mL
Dry white (or alcohol-free) wine	4 tsp.	20 mL

Process all 5 ingredients in blender, scraping sides down occasionally, until mixture is thick and paste-like. Add 1 tsp. (5 mL) wine if necessary, to help process. Basil should be very finely chopped. Makes ¼ cup (60 mL).

2 tsp. (10 mL): 52 Calories; 4.9 g Total Fat; 38 mg Sodium; 1 g Protein; 1 g Carbohydrate; trace Dietary Fiber

Pictured on page 89.

1. Asparagus Risotto, page 105
2. Gnocchi With Tomato Purée, page 103
3. Italian Vegetable Bowl, page 105

Props Courtesy Of: Stokes

RED CLAM SAUCE

Lots of tomato sauce with this instead of the more common light-colored sauce.

Chopped onion	1 cup	250 mL
Garlic cloves, minced	2	2
Olive oil	3 tbsp.	50 mL
Can of diced tomatoes, with juice	28 oz.	796 mL
Granulated sugar	1 tsp.	5 mL
Salt	1 tsp.	5 mL
Pepper	¼ tsp.	1 mL
Dried whole oregano	½ tsp.	2 mL
Dried sweet basil	1 tsp.	5 mL
Can of tomato paste	5½ oz.	156 mL
Red (or alcohol-free) wine	½ cup	125 mL
Reserved juice from clams		
Chopped fresh parsley	1 tbsp.	15 mL
Cans of baby clams (5 oz., 142 g, each), drained and juice reserved	2	2

Sauté onion and garlic in olive oil in large saucepan until onion is soft.

Add next 10 ingredients. Stir. Simmer, uncovered, for 10 minutes.

Add clams. Heat through. Makes 5½ cups (1.4 L).

½ **cup (125 mL):** *101 Calories; 4.4 g Total Fat; 455 mg Sodium; 6 g Protein; 9 g Carbohydrate; 2 g Dietary Fiber*

When buying clams or mussels in the shell, choose those shells that are tightly sealed or ones that close when tapped. After steaming, discard any unopened clams or mussels because this means that they were dead before cooking and are not to be eaten.

CLAMS IN WINE SAUCE

Not a thick sauce, but perfect to smother pasta in. Garnish with fresh parsley.

Cans of baby clams (5 oz., 142 g, each), drained and juice reserved	2	2
Dry white (or alcohol-free) wine	¼ cup	60 mL
Green onions, sliced	2	2
Dried sweet basil	1 tsp.	5 mL
Dried whole oregano, crushed	¼ tsp.	1 mL
Dried rosemary, crushed	¼ tsp.	1 mL
Sliced fresh mushrooms	1 cup	250 mL
Skim evaporated milk	1 cup	250 mL
Cornstarch	4 tsp.	20 mL
Non-fat spreadable cream cheese	2 tbsp.	30 mL

Combine reserved clam juice, wine, green onion, basil, oregano, rosemary and mushrooms in medium saucepan. Cover. Simmer for 15 minutes until mushrooms are soft.

Combine evaporated milk and cornstarch in small bowl. Add to mushroom mixture. Heat and stir until boiling and thickened. Stir in clams. Reduce heat. Simmer until hot. Remove from heat.

Add cream cheese. Stir until melted. Makes 3 cups (750 mL).

½ **cup (125 mL):** *101 Calories; 0.7 g Total Fat; 194 mg Sodium; 11 g Protein; 10 g Carbohydrate; trace Dietary Fiber*

MARINATED TOMATOES

Marinated tomatoes can be stored for up to two days in the refrigerator. Bring to room temperature before combining with pasta. This dish can also be served warm by gently heating in microwave oven or saucepan.

Ripe medium roma (plum) tomatoes, finely diced	6	6
Olive oil	4 tsp.	20 mL
Large garlic clove, minced	1	1
Finely chopped fresh sweet basil (or 2 tsp., 10 mL, dried)	2 tbsp.	30 mL
Tomato juice	¼ cup	60 mL
Lemon juice	2 tsp.	10 mL
Salt	½ tsp.	2 mL
Freshly ground pepper, sprinkle		

Combine all 8 ingredients in medium bowl. Stir well. Cover. Let stand at room temperature for at least 1 hour to allow flavors to blend. Makes 2 cups (500 mL).

½ cup (125 mL): 86 Calories; 5.2 g Total Fat; 413 mg Sodium; 2 g Protein; 10 g Carbohydrate; 2 g Dietary Fiber

Variation: Omit tomato juice and lemon juice and add ¼ cup (60 mL) dry white (or alcohol-free) wine.

TOMATO MEATBALL SAUCE

A perfect sauce if you're in the mood for spaghetti and meatballs!

Can of stewed tomatoes, with juice, chopped	28 oz.	796 mL
Can of tomato sauce	14 oz.	398 mL
Finely chopped onion	2 tbsp.	30 mL
Garlic cloves, minced	2	2
Whole cloves	10	10
Bay leaf	1	1
Dried sweet basil	1 tsp.	5 mL
Salt	½ tsp.	2 mL
Freshly ground pepper, sprinkle		
Lean ground beef	1 lb.	454 g
Bread slices, processed into crumbs	2	2
Frozen egg product, thawed	3 tbsp.	50 mL
Skim milk	⅓ cup	75 mL
Grated light Parmesan cheese	2 tbsp.	30 mL
Garlic powder	½ tsp.	2 mL
Dried whole oregano, crushed	½ tsp.	2 mL
Salt, sprinkle		
Freshly ground pepper, sprinkle		

Combine first 9 ingredients in large saucepan. Bring to a boil. Reduce heat. Simmer, partially covered, for 45 minutes.

Combine remaining 9 ingredients in medium bowl. Mix well. Form into 1 inch (2.5 cm) balls. Place on lightly greased baking sheet with sides. Bake in 400°F (205°C) oven for about 15 minutes. Drain. Blot meatballs with paper towel. Add meatballs to sauce. Simmer, partially covered, for 30 minutes. Discard bay leaf and cloves. Makes 6 cups (1.5 L).

¾ cup (175 mL): 163 Calories; 5.5 g Total Fat; 896 mg Sodium; 14 g Protein; 16 g Carbohydrate; 2 g Dietary Fiber

Pictured on page 89.

ROASTED PEPPER SAUCE

As a variation, try this with yellow, orange or green peppers. Serve over whole wheat or flavored pasta.

Large red peppers	5	5
Chopped fresh sweet basil	⅔ cup	150 mL
Garlic cloves, crushed	2	2
Green onions, thinly sliced	6	6
Margarine (or butter)	1 tsp.	5 mL
All-purpose flour	1½ tbsp.	25 mL
Can of skim evaporated milk	13½ oz.	385 mL
Dried whole oregano	½ tsp.	2 mL
Ground marjoram	½ tsp.	2 mL
Dried thyme	½ tsp.	2 mL
Salt	1½ tsp.	7 mL
Freshly ground pepper	½ tsp.	2 mL

Place peppers on baking sheet. Broil 3 inches (7.5 cm) from heat for 30 minutes, turning several times, until skin is blackened. Remove from oven. Cover with foil. Let stand until cool enough to handle. Peel off skin and discard seeds, reserving liquid.

Put peppers, reserved liquid and basil into blender. Process until very finely chopped.

Sauté garlic and green onion in margarine in non-stick frying pan until onion is soft.

Combine flour and evaporated milk in small cup until smooth. Add oregano, marjoram, thyme, salt and pepper. Stir. Add to garlic mixture. Add pepper purée. Heat, stirring occasionally, until sauce is boiling and thickened. Serve immediately. Makes 4½ cups (1.1 L).

1 cup (250 mL): 155 Calories; 1.6 g Total Fat; 1162 mg Sodium; 11 g Protein; 27 g Carbohydrate; 4 g Dietary Fiber

YELLOW PEPPER SAUCE

This can be served as an accompaniment or first course.

Garlic cloves, minced	2	2
Olive oil	1 tbsp.	15 mL
Water	⅓ cup	75 mL
Vegetable bouillon powder	1 tsp.	5 mL
Dried crushed chilies, just a pinch		
Very finely chopped red onion	½ cup	125 mL
Very finely chopped yellow pepper	2 cups	500 mL
Dried sweet basil	1 tsp.	5 mL
Salt	½ tsp.	2 mL
Chopped fresh parsley	2 tbsp.	30 mL

Sauté garlic in olive oil in large non-stick frying pan until soft. Add water, bouillon powder and chilies. Bring to a boil.

Add red onion, yellow pepper, basil and salt. Stir. Cover. Cook for 40 minutes, stirring occasionally, until onion and pepper are very soft. Stir in parsley. Makes about 1½ cups (375 mL).

⅔ cup (150 mL): 102 Calories; 3.8 g Total Fat; 491 mg Sodium; 3 g Protein; 15 g Carbohydrate; 2 g Dietary Fiber

Pictured on page 89.

For maximum flavor, add garlic at the end of the cooking time. For more subtle flavor, cook unpeeled garlic cloves whole.

Marinara Sauce

One of the popular pasta sauces. Red and spicy.

Chopped onion	1 cup	250 mL
Garlic cloves, minced	2-3	2-3
Olive oil	2 tbsp.	30 mL
Can of diced tomatoes, with juice	28 oz.	796 mL
Can of tomato paste	5½ oz.	156 mL
Granulated sugar	1 tbsp.	15 mL
Parsley flakes	2 tsp.	10 mL
Dried sweet basil	1½ tsp.	7 mL
Dried whole oregano	½ tsp.	2 mL
Salt	½ tsp.	2 mL

Sauté onion and garlic in olive oil in frying pan for about 5 minutes until onion is soft.

Add tomatoes, tomato paste, sugar, parsley flakes, basil, oregano and salt. Mix. Bring to a boil. Reduce heat. Simmer for about 15 minutes, stirring occasionally. Makes about 2⅔ cups (650 mL).

1 cup (250 mL): 138 Calories; 6.4 g Total Fat; 567 mg Sodium; 3 g Protein; 20 g Carbohydrate; 4 g Dietary Fiber

Three Tomato Sauce

Uses three kinds of fresh tomatoes—sun-dried, fresh, and canned. Serve over pasta or Polenta Wedges, page 33.

Medium onion, chopped	1	1
Garlic clove, crushed	1	1
Olive oil	1 tsp.	5 mL
Sun-dried tomato halves, quartered	8	8
Cans of roma (plum) tomatoes, (14 oz., 398 mL, each), with juice, processed	2	2
Finely chopped fresh sweet basil	¼ cup	60 mL
Medium roma (plum) tomatoes, diced	3	3

Sauté onion and garlic in olive oil in large non-stick frying pan until onion is soft.

Add next 3 ingredients. Bring to a boil, stirring occasionally.

Add roma tomato. Stir. Reduce heat. Simmer for 1 minute. Makes 4 cups (1 L).

¾ cup (175 mL): 82 Calories; 1.8 g Total Fat; 264 mg Sodium; 3 g Protein; 16 g Carbohydrate; 4 g Dietary Fiber

Mushroom and Asparagus Sauce

Serve with any kind of pasta you have in your cupboard.

Fresh asparagus, cut on diagonal into 1 inch (2.5 cm) lengths	1 lb.	454 g
Water	2 tbsp.	30 mL
Chopped onion	½ cup	125 mL
Garlic clove, minced	1	1
Margarine (or butter)	1 tsp.	5 mL
Sliced fresh mushrooms	3 cups	750 mL
Salt	¾ tsp.	4 mL
Freshly ground pepper, sprinkle		
Frozen egg product, thawed	6 tbsp.	100 mL
Skim evaporated milk	½ cup	125 mL
Grated light Parmesan cheese	2 tbsp.	30 mL

Place asparagus and water in 1 quart (1 L) microwave-safe casserole dish. Cover. Microwave on high (100%) for about 5 minutes until just tender. Drain. Transfer to serving bowl. Keep warm.

Sauté onion and garlic in margarine in medium non-stick frying pan for 2 minutes. Add mushrooms. Sauté for about 4 minutes. Cook until liquid is evaporated and mushrooms are golden. Add salt and pepper. Stir. Keep warm.

Beat egg product, evaporated milk and cheese together in small bowl. Add mushroom mixture to asparagus in serving bowl. Add egg product mixture. Stir to coat well. Makes 2¼ cups (550 mL).

⅔ cup (150 mL): 50 Calories; 0.8 g Total Fat; 332 mg Sodium; 6 g Protein; 7 g Carbohydrate; 2 g Dietary Fiber

Homemade Pasta

T ry one of these fresh pasta recipes and you'll have a hard time going back to the box for your spaghetti or macaroni. Basic Pasta Dough, page 97, will never let you down but for something with a bit more pizzazz, make Basil and Garlic Pasta Dough, page 98.

Egg Pasta Dough

Using egg product makes this a low-fat pasta.

All-purpose flour **(or durum semolina)**	**3 cups**	**750 mL**
Salt	**1 tsp.**	**5 mL**
Frozen egg product, **thawed**	**8 oz.**	**227 mL**
Warm water	**1-2 tbsp.**	**15-30 mL**

Place flour and salt in food processor or large bowl. Make a well in center.

With food processor running, gradually add egg product and warm water through feed tube until mixture forms ball. Or gradually stir into flour mixture in bowl until soft ball forms. Add bit more water if dough is too dry. Turn out onto lightly floured surface. Knead until smooth. Cover with plastic wrap. Let rest for 30 minutes. Roll out ¼ of dough very thin (about ⅛ inch, 1.5 mm) on lightly floured surface, dusting with all-purpose flour as needed to prevent sticking. Let stand for 10 minutes to dry. Flip over. Let stand for 10 minutes. Roll up loosely, jelly roll-style. To make noodles, use sharp knife to cut crosswise into ¼ inch (6 mm) slices. Toss gently to unroll. Sprinkle with bit of flour to prevent sticking. Toss. Repeat until all dough is used. Makes about 1½ lbs. (680 g).

3 oz. (85 g): 196 Calories; 0.7 g Total Fat; 395 mg Sodium; 8 g Protein; 38 g Carbohydrate; 2 g Dietary Fiber

Pictured on page 54.

BASIC PASTA DOUGH

Durum semolina can be found at most large grocery or specialty stores.

All-purpose flour (or durum semolina), approximately	3 cups	750 mL
Salt	1 tsp.	5 mL
Warm water, approximately	1 cup	250 mL

Place flour and salt in food processor or large bowl. Make a well in center.

With food processor running, gradually add warm water through feed tube until mixture forms ball. Or gradually stir into flour mixture in bowl until soft ball forms. Add bit more water if dough is too dry. Turn out onto lightly floured surface. Knead until smooth. Cover with plastic wrap. Let rest for 30 minutes. Roll out ¼ of dough very thin (about ¹⁄₁₆ inch, 1.5 mm) on lightly floured surface, dusting with all-purpose flour as needed to prevent sticking. Let stand for 10 minutes to dry. Flip over. Let stand for 10 minutes. Roll up loosely, jelly roll-style. To make noodles, use sharp knife to cut crosswise into ¼ inch (6 mm) slices. Toss gently to unroll. Sprinkle with bit of flour to prevent sticking. Toss. Repeat until all dough is used. Makes about 1½ lbs. (680 g).

3 oz. (85 g): *180 Calories; 0.5 g Total Fat; 340 mg Sodium; 5 g Protein; 38 g Carbohydrate; 2 g Dietary Fiber*

LASAGNA NOODLES: Roll out ½ of dough very thin (about ¹⁄₁₆ inch, 1.5 mm) on lightly floured surface. Cut into 2 x 10 inch (5 x 25 cm) strips. Proceed as above.

SOUP NOODLES: Roll out ¼ of dough very thin (about ¹⁄₁₆ inch, 1.5 mm) on lightly floured surface. Cut into long 4 inch (10 cm) wide strips. Let stand for 10 minutes to dry. Flip over. Dry for 10 minutes. Stack strips on top of one another. Cut with sharp knife angled one way and then the other to create irregularly shaped, short noodles.

Drain pasta well in a colander before tossing with sauce to avoid the sauce becoming diluted.

★★★★★★★★★★★★★★★★★★★★★★★★★★★★★★★★★

BASIL AND GARLIC PASTA DOUGH

Very tasty.

All-purpose flour (or durum semolina)	2 cups	500 mL
Salt	1 tsp.	5 mL
Garlic cloves, minced	5	5
Dried sweet basil, crushed	1 tsp.	5 mL
Frozen egg product, thawed	⅓ cup	75 mL
Warm water, approximately	⅓ cup	75 mL

Combine flour, salt, garlic and basil in food processor or large bowl.

Combine egg product and warm water in small cup. With food processor running, gradually add through feed tube until mixture forms ball. Or gradually stir into flour mixture in bowl until soft ball forms. Add bit more water if dough is too dry. Turn out onto lightly floured surface. Knead until smooth. Cover with plastic wrap. Let rest for 30 minutes. Roll out ¼ of dough very thin (about ¹⁄₁₆ inch, 1.5 mm) on lightly floured surface, dusting with all-purpose flour as needed to prevent sticking. Let stand for 10 minutes to dry. Flip over. Let stand for 10 minutes. Roll up loosely, jelly roll-style. To make noodles, use sharp knife to cut crosswise into ¼ inch (6 mm) slices. Toss gently to unroll. Sprinkle with bit of flour to prevent sticking. Toss. Repeat until all dough is used. Makes about 1 lb. (454 g).

3 oz. (85 g): *193 Calories; 0.6 g Total Fat; 540 mg Sodium; 7 g Protein; 39 g Carbohydrate; 2 g Dietary Fiber*

GREEN ONION PASTA DOUGH

A white dough with bits of green onion for color.

Green onions, chopped	3	3
Frozen egg product, thawed	⅓ cup	75 mL
Warm water, approximately	⅔ cup	150 mL
All-purpose flour (or durum semolina)	2½ cups	625 mL
Salt	1 tsp.	5 mL

Combine green onion, egg product and warm water in blender. Process until onion is very finely minced.

Combine flour and salt in food processor or large bowl. Make a well in center. With food processor running, gradually add onion mixture through feed tube until mixture forms ball. Or gradually stir into flour mixture in bowl until soft ball forms. Add bit more water if dough is too dry. Turn out onto lightly floured surface. Knead until smooth. Cover with plastic wrap. Let rest for 30 minutes. Roll out ½ of dough very thin (about ¹⁄₁₆ inch, 1.5 mm) on lightly floured surface, dusting with flour as needed to prevent sticking. Let stand for 10 minutes to dry. Flip over. Let stand for 10 minutes. Roll up loosely, jelly roll-style. To make noodles, use sharp knife to cut crosswise into ¼ inch (6 mm) slices. Toss gently to unroll. Sprinkle with bit of flour to prevent sticking. Toss. Repeat until all dough is used. Makes 1¼ lbs. (560 g).

3 oz. (85 g): *187 Calories; 0.6 g Total Fat; 432 mg Sodium; 7 g Protein; 38 g Carbohydrate; 2 g Dietary Fiber*

To prevent pasta from sticking, add oil to the cooking water. Or, stir occasionally during cooking to accomplish the same result.

LEMON PEPPER PASTA DOUGH

Great with a seafood a or wine sauce.

All-purpose flour (or durum semolina)	2½ cups	625 mL
Grated peel of 1 medium lemon		
Salt	1 tsp.	5 mL
Freshly ground pepper	1 tsp.	5 mL
Juice of 1 medium lemon, plus water to make	⅔ cup	150 mL
Frozen egg product, thawed	⅓ cup	75 mL

Combine flour, lemon peel, salt and pepper in food processor or large bowl. Make a well in center.

Combine lemon juice, water and egg product in small cup. With food processor running, gradually add through feed tube until mixture forms ball. Or gradually stir into flour mixture in bowl and mix until soft ball forms. Add bit more water if dough is too dry. Turn out onto lightly floured surface. Knead until smooth. Cover with plastic wrap. Let rest for 30 minutes. Roll out ½ of dough very thin (about ¹⁄₁₆ inch, 1.5 mm) on lightly floured surface, dusting with flour as needed to prevent sticking. Let stand for 10 minutes to dry. Flip over. Let stand for 10 minutes. Roll up loosely, jelly roll-style. To make noodles, use sharp knife to cut crosswise into ¼ inch (6 mm) slices. Toss gently to unroll. Sprinkle with bit of flour to prevent sticking. Toss. Repeat until all dough is used. Makes 1¼ lbs. (560 g).

3 oz. (85 g): 191 Calories; 0.6 g Total Fat; 432 mg Sodium; 7 g Protein; 40 g Carbohydrate; 2 g Dietary Fiber

CHILI PEPPER PASTA DOUGH

A subtle hint of heat.

All-purpose flour (or durum semolina)	2 cups	500 mL
Salt	1 tsp.	5 mL
Dried chilies, finely crushed	2 tsp.	10 mL
Frozen egg product, thawed	⅓ cup	75 mL
Tomato juice (or water), approximately	⅓ cup	75 mL

Combine flour, salt and chilies in food processor or large bowl.

Combine egg product and tomato juice in small cup. With food processor running, gradually add through feed tube until mixture forms ball. Or gradually stir into flour mixture in bowl until soft ball forms. Add bit more tomato juice if dough is too dry. Turn out onto lightly floured surface. Knead until smooth. Cover with plastic wrap. Let rest for 30 minutes. Roll out ½ of dough very thin (about ¹⁄₁₆ inch, 1.5 mm) on lightly floured surface, dusting with flour as needed to prevent sticking. Let stand for 10 minutes to dry. Flip over. Let stand for 10 minutes. Roll up loosely, jelly roll-style. To make noodles, use sharp knife and cut crosswise into ¼ inch (6 mm) slices. Toss gently to unroll. Repeat with remaining ½ of dough. Makes 1 lb. (454 g).

3 oz. (85 g): 193 Calories; 0.7 g Total Fat; 596 mg Sodium; 7 g Protein; 39 g Carbohydrate; 2 g Dietary Fiber

RAVIOLI

Here's a chance to make your own when you have some time to devote to cooking. Serve with Meat Sauce, page 60.

DOUGH

Large eggs	3	3
Olive oil	3 tbsp.	50 mL
All-purpose flour	3 cups	750 mL
Water	3-6 tbsp.	50-100 mL

BEEF FILLING

Lean ground beef	1 lb.	454 g
Finely chopped onion	⅓ cup	75 mL
Dry bread crumbs	⅓ cup	75 mL
Salt	1 tsp.	5 mL
Pepper	¼ tsp.	1 mL
Garlic powder	¼ tsp.	1 mL
Ground allspice	⅛ tsp.	0.5 mL
Frozen chopped spinach, cooked and squeezed dry	10 oz.	300 g
Grated Parmesan cheese	½ cup	125 mL

Dough: Beat eggs until frothy. Add olive oil, flour and smallest amount of water. Mix well to form fairly firm ball. Add water as needed. If dough gets too wet, add more flour. Turn out onto lightly floured surface. Knead until smooth. Cover. Let rest for 30 minutes.

Beef filling: Mix all 9 ingredients in bowl. If mixture seems too dry, add 1 egg. Chill until needed. Divide dough into 4 equal balls.

1. Roll each ball into paper-thin sheet.

2. On ½ place 1 tsp. (5 mL) filling about 1 inch (2.5 cm) apart to cover surface. Lay other ½ of sheet over top.

3. Press with fingers between each mound to seal.

4. Cut into 2 inch (5 cm) squares. Press each edge with fork to seal. Add, several at a time, to boiling water. Stir. Cook for 8 to 10 minutes until risen to top. Drain. Makes about 48 ravioli.

4 ravioli: 290 Calories; 12.2 g Total Fat; 387 mg Sodium; 15 g Protein; 29 g Carbohydrate; 2 g Dietary Fiber

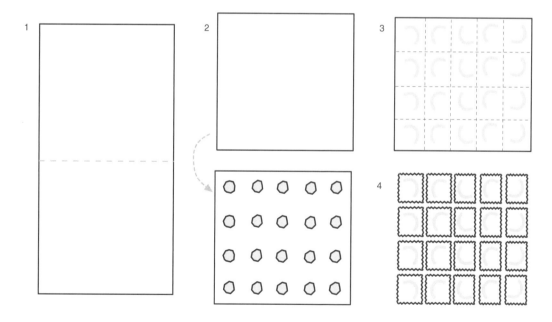

★★★★★★★★★★★★★★★★★★★★★★★★★★★★★★

Side Dishes

Serve one or two for supper, or more for a buffet. Regardless, these Italian side dishes are a pleasing accompaniment to meal. Colorful bell peppers take center stage in Grilled Peperonata, and herbed vegetables highlight shell pasta in Shells Primavera, both page 102. Eggplant Parmigiana, page 110 is easy to make-ahead, or you can savor the taste of garlic by making Italian Mushroom Grill, page 111.

ITALIAN SQUASH STIR-FRY

Spoon over rice or pasta or use as a vegetable accompaniment with any meat dish.

Olive oil	1 tbsp.	15 mL
Small green or yellow zucchini, cut in half lengthwise and then crosswise into ½ inch (12 mm) slices	4	4
Large red onion, slivered lengthwise	1	1
Thinly sliced fresh sweet basil	¼ cup	60 mL
Garlic clove, minced	1	1
Salt	1 tsp.	5 mL
Freshly ground pepper	⅛ tsp.	0.5 mL
Large roma (plum) tomatoes, sliced	6	6
Grated part-skim mozzarella cheese	1 cup	250 mL
Freshly grated Parmesan cheese (optional)		

Heat olive oil in large non-stick wok or frying pan until hot. Stir-fry zucchini and red onion for 3 to 5 minutes until tender-crisp. Stir in basil, garlic, salt and pepper.

Spread zucchini mixture evenly in bottom of wok. Lay tomato on zucchini. Sprinkle with mozzarella cheese. Cook, without stirring, for 2 minutes until cheese is melted. Garnish with Parmesan cheese. Serves 6.

1 serving: 123 Calories; 6.1 g Total Fat; 562 mg Sodium; 7 g Protein; 12 g Carbohydrate; 4 g Dietary Fiber

GRILLED PEPERONATA

Can be served as a side dish or tossed with pasta. The tangy balsamic vegetables are good either way.

Olive oil	3 tbsp.	50 mL
Garlic cloves, minced	2	2
Fresh rosemary leaves, chopped	2 tsp.	10 mL
Medium green pepper, halved	1	1
Medium red pepper, halved	1	1
Medium orange pepper, halved	1	1
Medium yellow pepper, halved	1	1
Large red onion, peeled and thickly sliced	1	1
Balsamic vinegar, to taste	2-4 tbsp.	30-60 mL
Chopped fresh parsley	1 tbsp.	15 mL

Combine olive oil, garlic and rosemary in small bowl. Let stand at room temperature for 30 minutes to allow flavors to blend.

Preheat lightly sprayed electric grill to high. Brush peppers and red onion with some of olive oil mixture. Cook on grill for 6 to 8 minutes, turning and brushing with olive oil mixture several times, until vegetables are tender-crisp. Remove to cutting board. Dice into ¾ inch (2 cm) pieces. Remove to large bowl.

Toss with vinegar and parsley. Makes about 6 cups (1.5 L).

½ cup (125 mL): 43 Calories; 3.5 g Total Fat; 1 mg Sodium; trace Protein; 3 g Carbohydrate; 1 g Dietary Fiber

SHELLS PRIMAVERA

Deliciously herbed vegetables.

Garlic clove, minced	1	1
Coarsely chopped onion	1 cup	250 mL
Olive oil	1 tbsp.	15 mL
Medium zucchini, with peel, diced	1	1
Diced green, red, orange or yellow pepper	1 cup	250 mL
Sliced fresh mushrooms	1 cup	250 mL
Can of diced tomatoes, drained	28 oz.	796 mL
Salt	½ tsp.	2 mL
Dried sweet basil	1 tsp.	5 mL
Granulated sugar	1 tsp.	5 mL
Dried whole oregano	¼ tsp.	1 mL
Ground thyme	¼ tsp.	1 mL
Large (not jumbo) shell pasta (about 8 oz., 225 g)	3 cups	750 mL
Boiling water	10 cups	2.5 L
Cooking oil (optional)	1 tbsp.	15 mL
Salt	2 tsp.	10 mL
Grated Parmesan cheese, sprinkle	2 tbsp.	30 mL

Sauté garlic and onion in olive oil in large non-stick frying pan for 4 minutes until onion is soft.

Add next 9 ingredients. Stir together well. Cover. Simmer for 15 minutes.

Cook pasta in boiling water, cooking oil and second amount of salt in large uncovered pot or Dutch oven for 10 to 12 minutes, stirring occasionally, until tender but firm. Drain. Return to pot. Pour vegetable mixture over top. Toss to coat well.

Sprinkle with Parmesan cheese. Serves 4.

1 serving: 359 Calories; 5.3 g Total Fat; 677 mg Sodium; 12 g Protein; 68 g Carbohydrate; 6 g Dietary Fiber

★★★★★★★★★★★★★★★★★★★★★★★★★★★★★★★

GNOCCHI

NYOH-kee is Italian for "dumplings." Use older potatoes, because they contain less water than new potatoes. Delicious served with Cheese Sauce With Bacon, page 91, Basil Pesto, page 91, or Bolognese Sauce, page 86. Here's two versions, one uses an egg and one makes more than the other.

Version 1

Potatoes (about 6 medium), 1½ lbs.		680 g
peeled and diced		
Water	2 cups	500 mL
Salt	2 tsp.	10 mL
All-purpose flour,	2½ cups	625 mL
approximately		

Cook potato, water and salt in medium saucepan until soft. Drain. Sieve hot potatoes into large bowl. Gradually stir in enough flour until stiff dough is formed. Roll pieces of dough into ropes, ½ to ¾ inch (12 to 20 mm) in diameter, on lightly floured surface. Cut ropes into 1 inch (2.5 cm) lengths. Makes about 120 gnocchi.

12 gnocchi: 223 Calories; 0.5 g Total Fat; 5 mg Sodium; 6 g Protein; 49 g Carbohydrate; 2 g Dietary Fiber

Version 2

Unpeeled potatoes	2 lbs.	900 g
Boiling water		
Large egg	1	1
Margarine (or butter),	2 tsp.	10 mL
softened		
All-purpose flour	2¼ cups	550 mL
Salt	1 tsp.	5 mL

Cook potatoes in boiling water in large saucepan until tender. Drain. Cool. Peel. Mash until no lumps remain. Make a well in center.

Add egg, margarine, flour and salt. Mix to make soft dough. Roll pieces of dough into ropes, ½ to ¾ inch (12 to 20 mm) in diameter, on lightly floured surface. Cut ropes into 1 inch (2.5 cm) lengths. Makes about 96 gnocchi.

12 gnocchi: 181 Calories; 1.6 g Total Fat; 290 mg Sodium; 5 g Protein; 37 g Carbohydrate; 2 g Dietary Fiber

GNOCCHI WITH TOMATO PURÉE

It takes a bit of time to make the gnocchi but no time at all for the sauce.

Gnocchi, this page	1½ lbs.	680 g
(full recipe)		
Water	16 cups	4 L
Salt	1 tbsp.	15 mL
Garlic clove, minced	1	1
Olive oil	¼ tsp.	1 mL
Can of roma (plum)	14 oz.	398 mL
tomatoes, with juice,		
processed		
Granulated sugar, pinch		
Salt, sprinkle (optional)		
Freshly ground pepper, sprinkle		
Chopped fresh sweet	1 tbsp.	15 mL
basil (or 1 tsp., 5 mL,		
dried)		
Grated light Parmesan	2 tbsp.	30 mL
cheese		
Grated part-skim	½ cup	125 mL
mozzarella cheese		
(optional)		

Simmer uncooked gnocchi, in 2 or 3 batches, in water and first amount of salt for about 6 minutes until they bob to surface and remain on top for 1 minute. Remove with slotted spoon to lightly greased 2 quart (2 L) casserole.

Sauté garlic in olive oil in small non-stick frying pan for about 30 seconds until soft. Add tomatoes, sugar, and second amount of salt and pepper. Boil, uncovered, for 5 minutes, until slightly reduced.

Stir in basil. Makes 1½ cups (375 mL).

Pour tomato purée over gnocchi. Sprinkle with both cheeses. Bake, uncovered, in 350°F (175°C) oven for about 20 minutes. Serves 8.

1 serving: 240 Calories; 1 g Total Fat; 115 mg Sodium; 7 g Protein; 51 g Carbohydrate; 3 g Dietary Fiber

Pictured on page 90.

RISOTTO MILANESE

This is prepared in a very different way than other rice. A lot of stirring produces a good product. From northern Italy. Serve with Osso Buco, page 57.

Boiling water	**8 cups**	**2 L**
Chicken bouillon cubes	**8**	**8**
(⅕ oz., 6 g, each), crumbled		

Saffron, just a pinch (to make yellow)

Finely chopped onion	**1 cup**	**250 mL**
Margarine (or butter)	**½ cup**	**125 mL**
Long grain white rice, uncooked	**2 cups**	**500 mL**
Grated Parmesan cheese	**½ cup**	**125 mL**
Margarine (or butter)	**2 tbsp.**	**30 mL**
Grated Parmesan cheese, heavy sprinkle		

Combine boiling water and bouillon cubes in large saucepan. Heat and stir until cubes are dissolved. Keep hot.

Measure ½ cup (125 mL) chicken broth into small saucepan. Add saffron. Heat and stir until dissolved.

Sauté onion in first amount of margarine in large saucepan until soft and lightly browned.

Add rice. Heat for 10 to 15 minutes, stirring constantly, until margarine is absorbed. Add 1 cup (250 mL) chicken broth. Heat, stirring constantly, until liquid is absorbed. Repeat 3 more times, stirring constantly, until total of 4 cups (1 L) chicken broth has been added and absorbed. Add saffron-broth mixture. Heat, stirring constantly, until absorbed.

Add first amount of cheese. Stir. Add remaining chicken broth, 1 cup (250 mL) at a time, stirring constantly, until rice is tender but firm. If rice is too dry after all broth has been used, add boiling water, ¼ cup (60 mL) at a time. Total cooking and stirring time is about 30 minutes.

Add second amount of margarine. Stir. Transfer to serving bowl. Sprinkle with second amount of Parmesan cheese. Serves 8.

*1 **serving**: 368 Calories; 18.3 g Total Fat; 1446 mg Sodium; 8 g Protein; 42 g Carbohydrate; 1 g Dietary Fiber*

RISOTTO

This Italian specialty requires stock to be added in portions while stirring constantly. A creamy rice dish that begs for Parmesan to be sprinkled on top.

Instant vegetable stock mix	**2 tbsp.**	**30 mL**
Boiling water	**5 cups**	**1.25 L**
Finely chopped onion	**1 cup**	**250 mL**
Margarine (or butter)	**2 tbsp.**	**30 mL**
Arborio rice (see Note), uncooked	**1½ cups**	**375 mL**
Red (or alcohol-free) wine	**2 tbsp.**	**30 mL**
Grated Parmesan cheese	**2 tbsp.**	**30 mL**

Stir stock mix into boiling water in large saucepan. Keep hot.

Sauté onion in margarine in separate large saucepan until soft.

Add rice. Heat and stir until margarine is absorbed.

Add 1 cup (250 mL) stock. Heat, stirring constantly until liquid is absorbed. Repeat 4 more times, stirring constantly, until remaining stock has been added, absorbed and rice is tender but firm. Total cooking and stirring time is about 25 minutes.

Add wine. Stir. Add cheese. Stir. Remove from heat. Makes 4 cups (1 L).

*½ **cup (125 mL)**: 200 Calories; 4.6 g Total Fat; 246 mg Sodium; 4 g Protein; 35 g Carbohydrate; 1 g Fiber*

Note: Italian Arborio rice is the kind needed for this recipe. If using Canadian or American short grain rice, you may need to add a little more vegetable stock.

ASPARAGUS RISOTTO

The secret is in the constant stirring. Best served immediately.

Olive oil	1 tbsp.	15 mL
Chopped onion	½ cup	125 mL
Sliced fresh mushrooms	1 cup	250 mL
Arborio rice, uncooked	1½ cups	375 mL
Grated lemon peel	2 tsp.	10 mL
Cans of condensed chicken broth (10 oz., 284 mL, each)	2	2
Water	1½ cups	375 mL
Dry white (or alcohol-free) wine	½ cup	125 mL
Cut fresh asparagus, 1 inch (2.5 cm) pieces	3 cups	750 mL
Water	⅓ cup	75 mL
Chopped fresh parsley, for garnish	1 tbsp.	15 mL
Grated lemon peel, for garnish	1 tbsp.	15 mL

Heat olive oil in large non-stick frying pan or wok. Sauté onion and mushrooms for 5 minutes until mushroom liquid is evaporated.

Stir in rice and lemon peel.

Combine chicken broth with first amount of water and wine. Add ½ cup (125 mL) broth mixture to rice. Cook, stirring constantly, until liquid is absorbed. Repeat 5 more times, stirring constantly. Add asparagus. Add remaining broth mixture, ¾ cup (175 mL) at a time, cooking and stirring constantly until liquid is absorbed and rice is tender and creamy.

Add second amount of water. Remove from heat. Sprinkle with parsley and lemon peel. Serve immediately. Makes 5 cups (1.25 L).

1 cup (250 mL): 335 Calories; 4.6 g Total Fat; 759 mg Sodium; 13 g Protein; 57 g Carbohydrate; 3 g Dietary Fiber

Pictured on page 90.

ITALIAN VEGETABLE BOWL

Lots of bright colors. Herbs and garlic come through nicely. To save time, have vegetables cut and measured ahead of time. Simply cook when ready.

Garlic clove, minced	1	1
Cooking oil	1 tsp.	5 mL
Sliced carrot, cut coin size	2 cups	500 mL
Water	2 tbsp.	30 mL
Broccoli florets	1 cup	250 mL
Cauliflower florets	1 cup	250 mL
Sliced zucchini, with peel	3 cups	750 mL
Dried sweet basil	1 tsp.	5 mL
Dried whole oregano	½ tsp.	2 mL
Water	3 tbsp.	50 mL
Can of diced tomatoes, drained	14 oz.	398 mL
Granulated sugar	½ tsp.	2 mL
Salt	¼ tsp.	1 mL
Pepper	⅛ tsp.	0.5 mL

Sauté garlic in cooking oil in non-stick frying pan until softened.

Add carrot and water. Cover. Cook for 3 minutes on medium-high.

Add next 6 ingredients. Cover. Cook for about 5 minutes until vegetables are tender-crisp. Do not overcook.

Add tomatoes, sugar, salt and pepper. Stir gently. Cover. Cook for about 1 minute until heated through. Makes 8 cups (2 L).

½ cup (125 mL): 22 Calories; 0.5 g Total Fat; 92 mg Sodium; 1 g Protein; 4 g Carbohydrate; 1 g Dietary Fiber

Pictured on page 90.

ZUCCHINI CASSEROLE

An excellent combination. Very good.

SAUCE

Chopped onion	1 cup	250 mL
Finely chopped celery	½ cup	125 mL
Margarine (or butter)	2 tbsp.	30 mL
Grated carrot	½ cup	125 mL
Can of diced tomatoes, with juice	14 oz.	398 mL
Can of tomato sauce	7½ oz.	213 mL
Granulated sugar	1 tsp.	5 mL
Dried sweet basil	½ tsp.	2 mL
Salt	½ tsp.	2 mL
Pepper	⅛ tsp.	0.5 mL
Medium zucchini, with peel	8	8

Olive oil, for frying

All-purpose flour	1 cup	250 mL
Large eggs, fork-beaten	2	2

Grated Romano cheese, sprinkle

Sauce: Sauté onion and celery in margarine in frying pan until soft.

Add next 7 ingredients. Simmer, uncovered, for about 20 to 25 minutes, stirring often, until thick.

Slice zucchini lengthwise into ½ inch (12 mm) thick slices.

Pour olive oil to ¼ inch (6 mm) depth in frying pan. Heat. Dip zucchini slices into flour, then into egg. Cook in olive oil, browning both sides until golden brown and fork-tender.

Layer sauce and zucchini in ungreased 3 quart (3 L) casserole. Sprinkle with cheese. Repeat with remaining zucchini and sauce. Top with sauce and cheese. Bake, uncovered, in 350°F (175°C) oven for about 20 minutes until hot and browned. Serves 8.

1 serving: 246 Calories; 14.3 g Total Fat; 480 mg Sodium; 7 g Protein; 25 g Carbohydrate; 5 g Dietary Fiber

NOODLES ALFREDO-STYLE

One of the quickest and easiest pasta plates.

Medium egg noodles	8 oz.	225 g
Cooking oil (optional)	1 tbsp.	15 mL
Salt	2 tsp.	10 mL
Boiling water	10 cups	2.5 L
Margarine (or butter)	¼ cup	60 mL
Grated Parmesan cheese	¼ cup	60 mL
Salt, sprinkle (optional)		

Grated Parmesan cheese, sprinkle

Cook noodles in cooking oil and first amount of salt in boiling water in large uncovered pot or Dutch oven for 5 to 7 minutes, stirring occasionally, until tender but firm. Drain. Return to pot.

Add margarine and first amount of Parmesan cheese. Heat and stir until margarine is absorbed and cheese is melted. Add second amount of salt to taste.

Sprinkle with second amount of Parmesan cheese. Makes 3 cups (750 mL).

1 cup (250 mL): 469 Calories; 20.3 g Total Fat; 230 mg Sodium; 12 g Protein; 60 g Carbohydrate; 2 g Dietary Fiber

1. Cassata Alla Siciliana, page 114
2. Bocconne Dolce, page 112

Props Courtesy Of: Stokes
The Bay

ITALIAN ZUCCHINI

One of the tastiest ways to enjoy zucchini.

Olive oil	2 tbsp.	30 mL
Balsamic vinegar	2 tbsp.	30 mL
Small garlic clove, minced	1	1
Salt	½ tsp.	2 mL
Freshly ground pepper, sprinkle		
Dried whole oregano, crushed	¼ tsp.	1 mL
Dried sweet basil, crushed	¼ tsp.	1 mL
Small zucchini (about 6 inches, 15 cm, long), with peel, cut on sharp diagonal to make 4 pieces each (for total of 16)	4	4

Whisk first 7 ingredients together in large container with lid. Makes ¼ cup (60 mL) marinade.

Add zucchini pieces. Cover. Toss to coat well. Marinate at room temperature for 30 minutes, tossing frequently. Preheat lightly sprayed electric grill to high. Remove zucchini, reserving marinade for basting. Place zucchini on grill. Cook for 5 to 6 minutes per side, basting with remaining marinade. Serves 4.

1 serving: 83 Calories; 7.1 g Total Fat; 344 mg Sodium; 2 g Protein; 5 g Carbohydrate; 2 g Dietary Fiber

NOODLES ROMANOFF

With cottage cheese, sour cream and spices, this is a simple casserole to make. Either cheese topping is good.

Broad egg noodles	8 oz.	225 g
Cooking oil (optional)	1 tbsp.	15 mL
Salt	2 tsp.	10 mL
Boiling water	10 cups	2.5 L
Creamed cottage cheese	1½ cups	375 mL
Sour cream	1 cup	250 mL
Green onions, chopped	8	8
Parsley flakes	1 tsp.	5 mL
Worcestershire sauce	1 tsp.	5 mL
Garlic salt	¼ tsp.	1 mL
Salt	½ tsp.	2 mL
Pepper	⅛ tsp.	0.5 mL
Grated medium Cheddar (or Parmesan) cheese	½ cup	125 mL

Cook noodles in cooking oil and first amount of salt in boiling water in large uncovered pot or Dutch oven for 5 to 7 minutes, stirring occasionally, until tender but firm. Drain. Return to pot.

Mix next 8 ingredients. Add to noodles. Stir. Turn into greased 2 quart (2 L) casserole.

Sprinkle Cheddar cheese over top. Cover. Bake in 350°F (175°C) oven for about 30 minutes. Serves 4.

1 serving: 463 Calories; 17.1 g Total Fat; 951 mg Sodium; 26 g Protein; 51 g Carbohydrate; 2 g Dietary Fiber

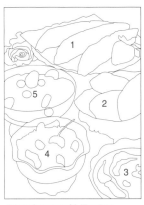

Props Courtesy Of: The Bay

1. Apricot Raisin Biscotti, page 118
2. Choco-Choco Chip Biscotti, page 117
3. Mocha Sorbetto, page 115
4. Ambrosia Dessert, page 116
5. Zabaglione, page 116

GORGONZOLA FLORENTINE

If Gorgonzola is not readily available, blue cheese may be used. Flavor is quite mild.

Fettuccine pasta	8 oz.	225 g
Cooking oil (optional)	1 tbsp.	15 mL
Salt	2 tsp.	10 mL
Boiling water	10 cups	2.5 L
Creamed cottage cheese	½ cup	125 mL
Frozen chopped spinach, cooked and squeezed dry	10 oz.	284 g
Grated Parmesan cheese	¼ cup	60 mL
Onion powder	¼ tsp.	1 mL
Whipping cream	1 cup	250 mL
Gorgonzola cheese, cut up	3 oz.	85 g
Salt, sprinkle (optional)		
Grated Parmesan cheese, sprinkle		

Cook fettuccine, in cooking oil and first amount of salt in boiling water in uncovered large pot or Dutch oven 5 to 7 minutes, stirring occasionally, until tender but firm. Drain. Return to pot.

Add next 4 ingredients. Heat on low.

Heat cream in small saucepan until boiling. Add Gorgonzola cheese and second amount of salt. Heat and stir until melted. Turn noodle mixture out onto warm plates or platter. Pour sauce over top.

Sprinkle with Parmesan cheese. Makes about 4½ cups (1.1 L).

1 cup (250 mL): 502 Calories; 26.4 g Total Fat; 546 mg Sodium; 20 g Protein; 47 g Carbohydrate; 3 g Dietary Fiber

---

Leftover whipped cream? Spoon dabs onto waxed paper on cookie sheet and freeze. Once frozen, store in sealable plastic bags. Thaw for about 10 minutes before serving on desserts.

EGGPLANT PARMIGIANA

Golden cheese layer on top. Assemble to the baking stage the day before or the morning of. Bake when needed.

Medium eggplants (about 2 lbs., 900 g), peeled and sliced	2	2
Salt	½ tsp.	2 mL
Boiling water		
All-purpose flour	½ cup	125 mL
Dried whole oregano	½ tsp.	2 mL
Dried sweet basil	½ tsp.	2 mL
Salt	½ tsp.	2 mL
Pepper	⅛ tsp.	0.5 mL
Cooking oil (or margarine or butter)	2 tbsp.	30 mL
Can of tomato sauce	14 oz.	398 mL
Process mozzarella cheese slices	8	8
Grated Parmesan cheese	½ cup	125 mL

Cook eggplant in first amount of salt in boiling water for 5 to 10 minutes. Should still be firm. Drain. Cool slightly.

Combine next 5 ingredients in small bowl.

Dip eggplant into flour mixture. Brown both sides in cooking oil in frying pan.

Pour tomato sauce into 2 quart (2 L) casserole to depth of ¼ inch (6 mm). Layer ⅓ of eggplant slices, ⅓ of remaining tomato sauce, ⅓ of mozzarella cheese and ⅓ of Parmesan cheese. Repeat twice with remaining egg plant, tomato sauce and cheeses. Cover. Bake in 400°F (205°C) oven for 20 minutes. Remove cover. Bake for 10 minutes. Serves 8.

1 serving: 218 Calories; 13.5 g Total Fat; 1034 mg Sodium; 12 g Protein; 13 g Carbohydrate; 2 g Dietary Fiber

ITALIAN MUSHROOM GRILL

Tastes like bruschetta in a mushroom. Excellent.

Water	⅓ cup	75 mL
Balsamic vinegar	2 tbsp.	30 mL
Garlic clove, minced	1	1
Dried sweet basil	1 tsp.	5 mL
Dried whole oregano	½ tsp.	2 mL
Salt, sprinkle		
Freshly ground pepper, sprinkle		
Large fresh portobello mushrooms, nicely shaped	4	4
Olive oil	4 tsp.	20 mL
Small roma (plum) tomatoes, seeded and chopped	2	2
Sliced green onion	¼ cup	60 mL
Grated Parmesan cheese	¼ cup	60 mL

Combine first 7 ingredients in small bowl. Makes 6 tbsp. (100 mL) marinade.

Remove stems from mushrooms and reserve for another purpose. Scrape and discard black "gills" from around underside of mushrooms with spoon. Place mushrooms in shallow casserole. Pour marinade over mushrooms. Marinate at room temperature for 30 minutes, turning over several times.

Preheat lightly sprayed electric grill to high. Drain mushrooms, reserving marinade for basting. Brush inside mushrooms with some olive oil. Place, oiled side down, on grill. Brush other side with remaining olive oil. Cook for 10 minutes, turning and basting several times surfaces with reserved marinade.

Remove to broiler pan. Discard any remaining marinade. Fill inside of mushrooms with tomato, green onion and cheese. Broil on top rack in oven for 2 to 3 minutes until cheese is melted and tomato is warm. Serves 4.

1 serving: 127 Calories; 7.4 g Total Fat; 137 mg Sodium; 7 g Protein; 12 g Carbohydrate; 3 g Dietary Fiber

PASTA CARBONARA

A bacon and egg pasta. Eggs are mixed into and then cooked by the hot pasta. A Roman favorite.

Spaghetti (or linguine) pasta	10 oz.	285 g
Cooking oil (optional)	1 tbsp.	15 mL
Salt	1 tbsp.	15 mL
Boiling water	12 cups	3 L
Bacon, cut crosswise into narrow strips	1 cup	250 mL
Egg yolks (large)	4	4
Whipping cream	2 tbsp.	30 mL
Grated Parmesan cheese	3 tbsp.	50 mL
Salt	½ tsp.	2 mL
Pepper	½ tsp.	2 mL
Grated Parmesan cheese	½ tsp.	2 mL

Cook spaghetti, in cooking oil and first amount of salt in boiling water in large uncovered pot or Dutch oven 11 to 13 minutes, stirring occasionally, until tender but firm. Drain.

Sauté bacon in frying pan. Drain. Add spaghetti. Stir to absorb flavor. Keep hot.

Beat egg yolks in heated bowl until light. Mix in cream, first amount of Parmesan cheese, second amount of salt and pepper. Stir. Turn spaghetti and bacon into egg mixture. Stir until hot pasta cooks eggs.

Sprinkle with second amount of Parmesan cheese. Serves 2.

1 serving: 553 Calories; 22.8 g Total Fat; 852 mg Sodium; 23 g Protein; 62 g Carbohydrate; 2 g Dietary Fiber

Desserts

The main course is over and the espresso is on. What better way to end an evening than with a sumptuous dessert? Serve decadent Italian Cheesecake, page 113, made with ricotta and mascarpone, an extra rich cream cheese.

Or finish on a lighter note with the cool taste of Lemon Sherbet, page 114, or Mocha Sorbetto, page 115.

BOCCONNE DOLCE

An Italian favorite that makes Sardi's famous. Meringue layers with chocolate, strawberries and cream.

MERINGUE

Egg whites (large), room temperature	6	6
Cream of tartar	¼ tsp.	1 mL
Granulated sugar	1½ cups	375 mL

FILLING

Semisweet chocolate chips	1 cup	250 mL
Water	3 tbsp.	50 mL
Whipping cream	3 cups	750 mL
Granulated sugar	5 tbsp.	75 mL
Vanilla	2 tsp.	10 mL
Fresh strawberries, sliced lengthwise (reserve a few whole for garnish)	3 cups	750 mL

Meringue: Beat egg whites and cream of tartar until soft peaks form. Gradually beat in sugar, until stiff and glossy. Line three 8 inch (20 cm) round pans with foil or outline three 8 inch (20 cm) circles on foil-lined cookie sheets. Grease foil very lightly. Divide and spread meringue evenly among pans. Bake in 250°F (120°C) oven for about 45 minutes until dry and crispy firm. Cool on racks. Peel off foil.

Filling: Melt chips with water in heavy saucepan on low. Spread over 2 meringue shells.

Whip cream, sugar and vanilla until stiff. Spread on all 3 meringue layers. Place 1 layer with chocolate on serving plate. Spoon ½ of strawberries over top. Place second layer with chocolate over first on plate. Spoon second ½ of strawberries over top. Add third layer. Garnish with whole berries. Chill for 4 to 5 hours before serving. Serves 8.

1 serving: 595 Calories; 37.1 g Total Fat; 90 mg Sodium; 6 g Protein; 65 g Carbohydrate; 2 g Dietary Fiber

Pictured on page 107.

ITALIAN CHEESECAKE

The cheese in this rich cake is ricotta and mascarpone, a double or triple cream cheese.

CRUST

Margarine (or butter)	**⅓ cup**	**75 mL**
Graham cracker crumbs	**1½ cups**	**375 mL**
Granulated sugar	**2 tbsp.**	**30 mL**
Cocoa, sifted if lumpy	**2 tbsp.**	**30 mL**

FILLING

Ricotta cheese, softened (see Note)	**1½ lbs.**	**680 g**
Mascarpone cheese (or cream cheese), softened	**8 oz.**	**225 g**
Granulated sugar	**1 cup**	**250 mL**
All-purpose flour	**2 tbsp.**	**30 mL**
Large eggs	**4**	**4**
Vanilla	**1½ tsp.**	**7 mL**
Cut glazed mixed fruit, chopped	**3 tbsp.**	**50 mL**
Semisweet chocolate baking squares (1 oz., 28 g, each), medium grated	**2**	**2**
Semisweet chocolate baking square, finely grated	**1 oz.**	**28 g**
Red and green candied cherries, halved, for garnish		

Crust: Melt margarine in medium saucepan. Stir in crumbs, sugar and cocoa until mixed. Press in bottom of ungreased 9 inch (22 cm) springform pan. Bake in 350°F (175°C) oven for about 10 minutes.

Filling: Combine ricotta cheese, mascarpone cheese, sugar and flour in medium bowl. Beat until mixed.

Add eggs, 1 at a time, beating slowly after each addition. Add vanilla. Mix.

Stir in mixed fruit and first amount of grated chocolate. Turn into pan. Bake in 350°F (175°C) oven for about 1 hour until set. Sprinkle with second amount of grated chocolate. Chocolate will melt. Cool. Garnish with cherry halves. Chill. Cuts into 8 wedges.

1 wedge: 644 Calories; 39.8 g Total Fat; 439 mg Sodium; 18 g Protein; 59 g Carbohydrate; 3 g Dietary Fiber

Pictured on front cover.

Note: If ricotta cheese isn't available use creamed cottage cheese. End result will be a bit softer.

YOGURT CHEESE

A wonderful substitute for cream cheese or sour cream. Chill in a covered container until the expiry date of the yogurt.

Plain skim milk yogurt (without gelatin)	**4 cups**	**1 L**

Line strainer with 2 layers of cheesecloth. Place over deep bowl. Spoon yogurt into strainer. Cover loosely with plastic wrap. Drain for 24 hours in refrigerator, discarding whey in bowl several times. Makes 2 cups (500 mL).

½ cup (125 mL): 131 Calories; 0.3 g Total Fat; 185 mg Sodium; 13 g Protein; 19 Carbohydrate; 0 g Dietary Fiber

To prevent cracks in a cheesecake, as soon as you remove it from the oven, place on a wire rack and run a knife around the inside edge of the pan. This also keeps the top even.

CASSATA ALLA SICILIANA

A special cake very unique in flavor. Excellent.

CAKE

Large eggs	3	3
Granulated sugar	1½ cups	375 mL
Vanilla	1 tsp.	5 mL
All-purpose flour	1½ cups	375 mL
Baking powder	1½ tsp.	7 mL
Salt	½ tsp.	2 mL
Margarine (or butter), melted	2 tbsp.	30 mL
Hot water	¾ cup	175 mL

RICOTTA FILLING

Ricotta cheese, room temperature	1 lb.	454 g
Granulated sugar	⅓ cup	75 mL
Milk	1 tbsp.	15 mL
Orange flavoring	1 tsp.	5 mL
Cut glazed mixed fruit, chopped	½ cup	125 mL
Semisweet chocolate chips, chopped	⅓ cup	75 mL

ICING

Semisweet chocolate chips	1 cup	250 mL
Water	3 tbsp.	50 mL
Orange flavoring	1 tsp.	5 mL
Margarine (or butter)	½ cup	125 mL
Icing (confectioner's) sugar	1½ cups	375 mL

Cake: Beat eggs in medium bowl until well blended. Beat in sugar, about 1½ tbsp. (25 mL) at a time. Add vanilla.

Add flour, baking powder and salt. Mix.

Melt margarine in hot water in cup. Stir into batter. Pour into 2 greased 8 inch (20 cm) round layer pans. Bake in 350°F (175°C) oven for 25 to 30 minutes until wooden pick inserted in center comes out clean. Cool. Slice each layer in half, lengthwise, to make total of 4 layers.

Ricotta Filling: Break up ricotta cheese in medium bowl. Add sugar, milk and orange flavoring. Beat until smooth. Add more milk, as needed, to reach spreading consistency.

Add fruit and chocolate chips. Mix. Divide and spread on 3 cake layers. Stack layers.

Icing: Combine first 4 ingredients in saucepan. Heat on low, stirring often, until chocolate chips are melted. Remove from heat.

Add icing sugar. Stir. Ice top and sides of cake. Icing will become firm fairly quickly. Serves 8 to 10.

1 serving: 796 Calories; 33.5 g Total Fat; 436 mg Sodium; 13 g Protein; 117 g Carbohydrate; 3 g Dietary Fiber

Pictured on page 107.

LEMON SHERBET

Serve small scoops for a light, cool dessert. Recipe doubles nicely if you want larger servings.

Yogurt Cheese, page 113	1½ cups	375 mL
Granulated sugar	1 cup	250 mL
Juice and grated peel of 1 medium lemon		
Frozen whipped topping, thawed	½ cup	125 mL

Beat Yogurt Cheese, sugar, lemon juice and lemon peel together on low until smooth.

Fold in whipped topping. Pour into 8 x 8 inch (20 x 20 cm) pan. Freeze for 8 hours or overnight until firm. Makes 2½ cups (625 mL).

½ cup (125 mL): 270 Calories; 2.2 g Total Fat; 114 mg Sodium; 8 g Protein; 57 g Carbohydrate; 1 g Dietary Fiber

TIRAMISU

A low-fat version of the original! Store this in the freezer and take out as needed.

Non-fat spreadable cream cheese 8 oz.		225 g
Yogurt Cheese, page 113	½ cup	125 mL
Icing (confectioner's) sugar, sifted	¾ cup	175 mL
Envelope of dessert topping mix	1	1
Skim milk	½ cup	125 mL
Granulated sugar	⅓ cup	75 mL
Water	3 tbsp.	50 mL
Egg whites (large)	2	2
Ladyfingers, approximately	40	40
Hot double-strength prepared coffee	¾ cup	175 mL
Granulated sugar	1 tbsp.	15 mL
Kahlúa liqueur	3 tbsp.	50 mL
Cocoa	1-2 tsp.	5-10 mL

Beat cream cheese, Yogurt Cheese and icing sugar together in large bowl until smooth.

Beat dessert topping and skim milk together according to package directions. Fold ½ of dessert topping into cheese mixture.

Combine granulated sugar, water and egg whites in top of double boiler over simmering water. Beat on high, over simmering water, until stiff peaks form. Gently fold into cheese mixture. Set aside.

Lay ½ of ladyfingers in single layer in bottom of foil-lined 9 x 9 inch (22 x 22 cm) pan.

Combine coffee, sugar and Kahlúa. Drizzle ½ of coffee mixture over ladyfingers. Spread with ½ of cheese mixture. Repeat with another layer of ladyfingers, coffee mixture and cheese mixture.

Top with thin layer of remaining ½ of dessert topping. Lightly sprinkle with cocoa. Freeze for about 2 hours. Cuts into 12 pieces.

1 piece: 204 Calories; 3.2 g Total Fat; 51 mg Sodium; 5 g Protein; 37 g Carbohydrate; trace Dietary Fiber

MOCHA SORBETTO

Sorbetto is the Italian word for sherbet. After the initial 45 minutes freezing time, the espresso mixture can be completed in an ice-cream maker.

Hot espresso (or double-strength regular) coffee	3½ cups	875 mL
Granulated sugar	⅔ cup	150 mL
Cocoa, sifted if lumpy	2 tbsp.	30 mL
Can of skim evaporated milk	13½ oz.	385 mL

Chill 9 x 13 inch (22 x 33 cm) pan in freezer. Pour coffee into medium bowl.

Combine sugar and cocoa in small bowl. Add to hot coffee. Beat together until dissolved.

Stir in evaporated milk. Pour into cold pan. Freeze for 45 minutes. Stir, bringing any crystals to center. Freeze for about 2 hours until hard. Use fork to break into chunks. Process in food processor until smooth. Freeze until serving time. Makes 8 cups (2 L).

½ cup (125 mL): 58 Calories; 0.1 g Total Fat; 33 mg Sodium; 2 g Protein; 13 g Carbohydrate; trace Dietary Fiber

Pictured on page 108.

Mark an X on the last few eggs in your refrigerator so that you know which ones to use first when you buy more.

AMBROSIA DESSERT

This dessert is best eaten within three hours.
Creamy white and very fruity.

Orzo pasta	½ cup	125 mL
Boiling water	2 cups	500 mL
Salt	½ tsp.	2 mL
Can of fruit cocktail, with juice	14 oz.	398 mL
Miniature marshmallows	2 cups	500 mL
Maraschino cherries, drained and cut into quarters	5	5
Small banana, diced	1	1
Envelope of dessert topping mix	1	1
Skim milk	⅓ cup	75 mL
Almond flavoring (or vanilla)	½ tsp.	2 mL
Toasted sliced almonds (optional)	2 tbsp.	30 mL
Maraschino cherries, with stems		

Cook pasta in boiling water and salt in medium saucepan for about 10 minutes, stirring occasionally, until tender but firm. Drain. Rinse with cold water. Drain.

Combine fruit cocktail with juice, marshmallows, cherries and banana in large bowl. Stir in pasta. Cover. Chill for 2 hours until juice is absorbed.

Beat dessert topping, milk and almond flavoring together in small bowl on high for about 2 minutes until very stiff. Fold into fruit mixture.

Sprinkle individual servings with almonds and garnish with maraschino cherries before serving. Makes 6 cups (1.5 L).

1 cup (250 mL): 224 Calories; 3.2 g Total Fat; 34 mg Sodium; 4 g Protein; 46 g Carbohydrate; 2 g Dietary Fiber

Pictured on page 108.

ZABAGLIONE

A special, light dessert. Serve warm or cold over assorted berries.

Egg yolks (large)	6	6
Granulated sugar	⅓ cup	75 mL
Marsala wine (or sherry)	¾ cup	175 mL

Combine egg yolks and sugar in top part of large (7 cup, 1.6 L) double boiler. Beat until lemon-colored and light.

Add wine. Mix. Place over simmering water. Be sure water in bottom pan doesn't touch top pan. Cook, beating constantly, until frothy, increased in volume, thickened and forms soft mound. Makes 4 cups (1 L).

½ cup (125 mL): 95 Calories; 3.8 g Total Fat; 7 mg Sodium; 2 g Protein; 9 g Carbohydrate; 0 g Dietary Fiber

Pictured on page 108.

Wine needs the right amount of cooking time to evaporate the alcohol. The flavor, acidity and sweetness of the wine comes through, without the alcohol. Boil a sauce for about 2 minutes, or simmer for about 15 minutes.

Choco-Choco Chip Biscotti

A great variation to the very popular almond biscotti.

All-purpose flour	2 cups	500 mL
Granulated sugar	1 cup	250 mL
Baking soda	1 tsp.	5 mL
Salt	⅛ tsp.	0.5 mL
Cocoa, sifted if lumpy	½ cup	125 mL
Mini semisweet chocolate chips	½ cup	125 mL
Large eggs	2	2
Egg whites (large)	2	2
Vanilla	1 tsp.	5 mL
Crème de Cacao (or milk)	1 tbsp.	15 mL

Combine first 6 ingredients in large bowl.

Combine eggs, egg whites, vanilla and Crème de Cacao in medium bowl. Beat with fork. Add to flour mixture. Mix. Dough will feel slightly dry. Turn out onto lightly floured surface. Knead gently 8 to 10 times. Form into 16 inch (40 cm) oval roll, 1½ inches (3.8 cm) thick at center. Place on lightly greased baking sheet. Bake in 350°F (175°C) oven for 30 minutes. Cool on wire rack for 10 minutes. Reduce heat to 325°F (160°C). Cut, slightly on diagonal, into ½ inch (12 mm) slices. Bake, cut side down, on baking sheet for 10 to 12 minutes. Turn over. Bake for 10 to 12 minutes until crisp. May be slightly soft in center but will harden when cooled. Remove to wire rack to cool. Makes 24 biscotti.

1 biscotti: 108 Calories; 2.2 g Total Fat; 83 mg Sodium; 3 g Protein; 21 g Carbohydrate; 1 g Dietary Fiber

Pictured on page 108.

Apricot Raisin Biscotti

This biscotti is a little wider than the others because of the bulk of the fruit.

All-purpose flour	2½ cups	625 mL
Granulated sugar	1 cup	250 mL
Baking soda	1 tsp.	5 mL
Salt	⅛ tsp.	0.5 mL
Large eggs	2	2
Egg whites (large)	2	2
Almond flavoring	½ tsp.	2 mL
Finely chopped dried apricots	¾ cup	175 mL
Chopped raisins	¾ cup	175 mL
Prepared orange juice	4 tsp.	20 mL

Combine flour, sugar, baking soda and salt in large bowl.

Combine next 6 ingredients in medium bowl. Beat with fork. Add to dry mixture. Mix. Dough will feel slightly dry. Turn out onto lightly floured surface. Knead gently 8 to 10 times. Form into 16 inch (40 cm) oval roll, 1½ inches (3.8 cm) thick at center. Place on lightly greased baking sheet. Bake in 350°F (175°C) oven for 30 minutes. Cool on wire rack for 10 minutes. Cut, slightly on diagonal, into ½ inch (12 mm) slices. Reduce heat to 325°F (160°C). Bake, cut side down, on baking sheet for 10 to 12 minutes. Turn over. Bake for 10 to 12 minutes until golden. May be slightly soft in center but will harden when cooled. Remove to wire rack to cool. Makes 24 biscotti.

1 biscotti: 111 Calories; 0.6 g Total Fat; 83 mg Sodium; 2 g Protein; 25 g Carbohydrate; 1 g Dietary Fiber

Pictured on page 108.

measurement tables

*T*hroughout this book measurements are given in Conventional and Metric measure. To compensate for differences between the two measurements due to rounding, a full metric measure is not always used. The cup used is the standard 8 fluid ounce. Temperature is given in degrees Fahrenheit and Celsius. Baking pan measurements are in inches and centimetres as well as quarts and litres. An exact metric conversion is given below as well as the working equivalent (Standard Measure).

OVEN TEMPERATURES

Fahrenheit (°F)	Celsius (°C)
175°	80°
200°	95°
225°	110°
250°	120°
275°	140°
300°	150°
325°	160°
350°	175°
375°	190°
400°	205°
425°	220°
450°	230°
475°	240°
500°	260°

PANS

Conventional Inches	Metric Centimetres
8x8 inch	20x20 cm
9x9 inch	22x22 cm
9x13 inch	22x33 cm
10x15 inch	25x38 cm
11x17 inch	28x43 cm
8x2 inch round	20x5 cm
9x2 inch round	22x5 cm
10x4$^{1}/_{2}$ inch tube	25x11 cm
8x4x3 inch loaf	20x10x7.5 cm
9x5x3 inch loaf	22x12.5x7.5 cm

SPOONS

Conventional Measure	Metric Exact Conversion Millilitre (mL)	Metric Standard Measure Millilitre (mL)
$^{1}/_{8}$ teaspoon (tsp.)	0.6 mL	0.5 mL
$^{1}/_{4}$ teaspoon (tsp.)	1.2 mL	1 mL
$^{1}/_{2}$ teaspoon (tsp.)	2.4 mL	2 mL
1 teaspoon (tsp.)	4.7 mL	5 mL
2 teaspoons (tsp.)	9.4 mL	10 mL
1 tablespoon (tbsp.)	14.2 mL	15 mL

CUPS

$^{1}/_{4}$ cup (4 tbsp.)	56.8 mL	60 mL
$^{1}/_{3}$ cup (5$^{1}/_{3}$ tbsp.)	75.6 mL	75 mL
$^{1}/_{2}$ cup (8 tbsp.)	113.7 mL	125 mL
$^{2}/_{3}$ cup (10$^{2}/_{3}$ tbsp.)	151.2 mL	150 mL
$^{3}/_{4}$ cup (12 tbsp.)	170.5 mL	175 mL
1 cup (16 tbsp.)	227.3 mL	250 mL
4$^{1}/_{2}$ cups	1022.9 mL	1000 mL (1 L)

DRY MEASUREMENTS

Conventional Measure Ounces (oz.)	Metric Exact Conversion Grams (g)	Metric Standard Measure Grams (g)
1 oz.	28.3 g	28 g
2 oz.	56.7 g	57 g
3 oz.	85.0 g	85 g
4 oz.	113.4 g	125 g
5 oz.	141.7 g	140 g
6 oz.	170.1 g	170 g
7 oz.	198.4 g	200 g
8 oz.	226.8 g	250 g
16 oz.	453.6 g	500 g
32 oz.	907.2 g	1000 g (1 kg)

CASSEROLES (CANADA & BRITAIN)

Standard Size Casserole	Exact Metric Measure
1 qt. (5 cups)	1.13 L
1$^{1}/_{2}$ qts. (7$^{1}/_{2}$ cups)	1.69 L
2 qts. (10 cups)	2.25 L
2$^{1}/_{2}$ qts. (12$^{1}/_{2}$ cups)	2.81 L
3 qts. (15 cups)	3.38 L
4 qts. (20 cups)	4.5 L
5 qts. (25 cups)	5.63 L

CASSEROLES (UNITED STATES)

Standard Size Casserole	Exact Metric Measure
1 qt. (4 cups)	900 mL
1$^{1}/_{2}$ qts. (6 cups)	1.35 L
2 qts. (8 cups)	1.8 L
2$^{1}/_{2}$ qts. (10 cups)	2.25 L
3 qts. (12 cups)	2.7 L
4 qts. (16 cups)	3.6 L
5 qts. (20 cups)	4.5 L

index

Company's Coming cookbooks are available at retail locations throughout Canada!

See mail order form

Buy any 2 cookbooks—choose a 3rd FREE of equal or less value than the lowest price paid.   *Available in French

Original Series		**CA$15.99 Canada**		**US$12.99 USA & International**	
CODE		**CODE**		**CODE**	
SQ	150 Delicious Squares*	CT	Cooking For Two*	CCBE	The Beef Book
CA	Casseroles*	BB	Breakfasts & Brunches*	ASI	Asian Cooking
MU	Muffins & More*	SC	Slow Cooker Recipes*	CB	The Cheese Book
SA	Salads*	ODM	One Dish Meals*	RC	The Rookie Cook
AP	Appetizers	ST	Starters*	RHR	Rush-Hour Recipes
SS	Soups & Sandwiches	SF	Stir-Fry*	SW	Sweet Cravings
CO	Cookies*	MAM	Make-Ahead Meals*	YRG	Year-Round Grilling
PA	Pasta*	PB	The Potato Book*	GG	Garden Greens
BA	Barbecues*	CCLFC	Low-Fat Cooking*	CHC	Chinese Cooking
PR	Preserves*	CCLFP	Low-Fat Pasta*	PK	The Pork Book
CH	Chicken, Etc.*	CFK	Cook For Kids	RL	Recipes For Leftovers
KC	Kids Cooking	SCH	Stews, Chilies & Chowders	EB	The Egg Book ◀NEW▶
		FD	Fondues		*May 1/04*

Greatest Hits Series

CODE	CA$12.99 Canada US$9.99 USA & International
ITAL	Italian
MEX	Mexican

Most Loved Recipe Collection

CODE	CA$23.99 Canada US$19.99 USA & International
MLA	Most Loved Appetizers
MLMC	Most Loved Main Courses ◀NEW▶
	April 1/04

Lifestyle Series

CODE	CA$17.99 Canada US$15.99 USA & International
GR	Grilling
DC	Diabetic Cooking

CODE	CA$19.99 Canada US$15.99 USA & International
HC	Heart-Friendly Cooking
DDI	Diabetic Dinners

Special Occasion Series

CODE	CA$20.99 Canada US$19.99 USA & International
GFK	Gifts from the Kitchen
CFS	Cooking for the Seasons

CODE	CA$22.99 Canada US$19.99 USA & International
WC	Weekend Cooking

CODE	CA$25.99 Canada US$22.99 USA & International
HFH	Home for the Holidays
DD	Decadent Desserts

Company's Coming COOKBOOKS®

companyscoming.com
visit our ↖ website

COMPANY'S COMING PUBLISHING LIMITED
2311 - 96 Street
Edmonton, Alberta, Canada T6N 1G3
Tel: (780) 450-6223 Fax: (780) 450-1857

Mail Order Form

See reverse for list of cookbooks

QUANTITY	CODE	TITLE	PRICE EACH	PRICE TOTAL
			$	$

DON'T FORGET to indicate your FREE book(s). (see exclusive mail order offer above) PLEASE PRINT

	TOTAL BOOKS (including FREE)		TOTAL BOOKS PURCHASED:	$

	INTERNATIONAL	CANADA & USA
Plus Shipping & Handling (PER DESTINATION)	$ 7.00 (one book)	$ 5.00 (1-3 books)
Additional Books (INCLUDING FREE BOOKS)	$ ($2.00 each)	$ ($1.00 each)
SUB-TOTAL	$	$
Canadian residents add G.S.T(7%)		$
TOTAL AMOUNT ENCLOSED	$	$

The Fine Print

- Orders outside Canada must be **PAID IN US FUNDS** by cheque or money order drawn on Canadian or US bank or by credit card.
- Make cheque or money order payable to: **COMPANY'S COMING PUBLISHING LIMITED.**
- Prices are expressed in Canadian dollars for Canada, US dollars for USA & International and are subject to change without prior notice.
- Orders are shipped surface mail. For courier rates, visit our web-site: **www.companyscoming.com** or contact us: **Tel: (780) 450-6223 Fax: (780) 450-1857.**
- Sorry, no C.O.D's.

☐ MasterCard   ☐ VISA

Expiry date _____

Account # _____

Name of cardholder _____

Cardholder's signature _____

Shipping Address

Send the cookbooks listed above to:

Name: _____

Street: _____

City: _____ Prov./State: _____

Country: _____ Postal Code/Zip: _____

Tel: ( ) _____

E-mail address: _____

Gift Giving

- Let us help you with your gift giving!
- We will send cookbooks directly to the recipients of your choice if you give us their names and addresses.
- Please specify the titles you wish to send to each person.
- If you would like to include your personal note or card, we will be pleased to enclose it with your gift order.
- Company's Coming Cookbooks make excellent gifts: Birthdays, bridal showers, Mother's Day, Father's Day, graduation or any occasion... collect them all!